God, I'm Serious This Time.

By Whittney Kilgore

Copyright © 2024 Whittney Kilgore
All rights reserved.
ISBN: 979-8-89480-873-4

Foreword

As we travel through the journey of life, we find ourselves influenced by the teachings, lifestyles, and experiences of others. They shape how we think of ourselves and one another. As children under the guardianship of parents, uncles, aunts, cousins, and friends, we imitated the culture and character of those around us. They taught us what was passed down to them, so we became infused with many of the same behaviors. Whether you grew up on a farm, in a beautiful home, or in city housing projects, the things you saw daily probably became normalized, whether they were morally good or bad. If the neighborhood was drug-infested, you were likely to experiment with drugs. If you grew up in a family where all the women were single parents, there was a strong possibility that your decisions would also put you at risk of being a single parent.

If you have patterns of lacking vision for your life, mediocrity, low self-esteem, and slothfulness, please know that these traits have an origin. Sexual perversion has also led women into lifestyles that result in toxic relationships. We won't even begin to discuss the unwanted pregnancies that stem from these indulgences. This all leads to your soul being inflicted with idolatry that produces guilt, shame, and dishonor. The enemy is an ancient adversary. He has capitalized on God's creation and is determined to damage us by any means necessary. We have authority over the enemy, so he first goes after your mind. This is why so many of God's people cannot be serious concerning their relationship with God. We have been bewitched. It's time to wake up! God has already given us a way of escape—Jesus Christ! He yearns to have an intimate relationship with us. When you follow Christ, obey His will, and believe His Word, you will find success, victory, peace, and wholesome relationships. "Submit yourselves therefore to God. Resist the devil, and he will flee from you." (James 4:7).

If you take some time to reflect honestly, you'll realize how your past environment affected you. Some of us are still fighting against the effects of those influences today. The Bible teaches us to trust God and lean not on our own understanding. Remember, never give your past permission to direct your future. God knows what others have done to you. He also knows what you have done to others. Forgive your enemies! You will need the same forgiveness extended to you. If you do not forgive, it will hold you hostage in mind, body, and soul, especially if these experiences were unhealthy, unrighteous, unjust, unholy, unloving, and undeserved. We must rehearse in our minds repeatedly to establish muscle memory, declaring that we are healed, delivered, and free.

There was a time in my life when I had to go ghost. I had to escape from my family to allow God to reconstruct my story. Some acquaintances may not mean you any good. Some friends may keep you from prospering. I say to you, separate yourself from them and focus your life on Christ Jesus. He is the Way! BE SERIOUS AND OF GOOD COURAGE.

Love,

Pastor Sabrina Nero

Introduction

How many times have you told God that you were ready to live for Him? You told Him that you were ready to change and get serious about your relationship with Him, only to end up in the same situations that had you crying out before. Sis, you are not alone! We've all been there, but the truth is that some people never get out of that cycle. Yeah, we want to change (I wanted to change too), but somehow, after the emotions subside, we end up back in toxic relationships, overeating our favorite unhealthy foods, doubting our potential, using the same nasty language, and focusing on everything but what God wants us to focus on. God desires for us to truly get to know Him. Don't beat yourself up too bad, though, because the same thing happened to the men who walked with Jesus. Paul said, *"I know the law but still can't keep it, and if the power of sin within me keeps sabotaging my best intentions, I obviously need help! I realize that I don't have what it takes. I can will it, but I can't do it. I decide to do good, but I don't really do it; I decide not to do bad, but then I do it anyway. My decisions, such as they are, don't result in actions. Something has gone wrong deep within me and gets the better of me every time." (Romans 7:17-20 The Message).* Paul was struggling to figure out this God thing too... but eventually, he came to find that the power to truly change came from living life on God's terms. Sis... that means a whole lifestyle change!

I know... I know. Shifting your whole lifestyle sounds like a bit much, but it's possible through Christ. My prayer is that as you read this book and make a personal commitment to **Do The Work**, you'll hear the Holy Spirit more clearly. I want you to have practical steps for really living a submitted life in a way that feels right for you. I believe that you'll become hungry for God and realize how much better life is on His terms. I'm praying that you'll finally move your emotions out of the way and say to God, "I'm serious this time!" and mean it. Not only will you declare it, but your life will produce spiritual fruit as a sign that He is truly working in your life.

Before we even start this journey, I need to make sure you have access to the most important person in this process: the Holy Spirit. We can do nothing meaningful apart from Him. Sis, if you've felt God calling you but haven't answered, this is your moment. You can read this book, but if you haven't accepted Jesus Christ as your Lord and Savior, you'll still be doing life on your own terms. The Bible says in Romans 10:9 that if you declare with your mouth, "Jesus is Lord," and believe in your heart that God raised him from the dead, you will be saved. As we begin this journey toward our confession, "God, I'm serious this time," let's take a moment to make sure that we are in right standing with God. Regardless of how much family you had before this confession, you now have a whole gang of sisters and brothers in Christ who are on the same mission: to find and live out their purpose in God, and enjoy life while doing it.

Welcome to the family, Sis!

Table of Contents

Foreword iii
Introduction vi
Table of Contents ix
Chapter 1 .... **1**
   How Did I Get Here? 1
Chapter 2 .... **15**
   Self-Sabotage... Am I Doing This to Myself? 15
Chapter 3 .... **37**
   Shaped by the "Culture" 37
Chapter 4 .... **67**
   Becoming the New You... 67
Chapter 5 .... **100**
   Sneaky Things That Hinder Your Growth 100
Chapter 6 .... **135**
   What is a Godly Woman ? 135
Chapter 7 .... **173**
   It's Serious This Time... Period! 173
   REFERENCES 201

Chapter 1

How Did I Get Here?

It's like you wake up one day, and Boom! You're a whole adult living a life that doesn't quite look like what you envisioned, and all of a sudden, feelings of disappointment creep in. Oh, and then you pick up your phone, hit the little blue app to take your mind off your disappointment, just to see all your classmates living their "best lives". Sometimes, we get so caught up in trying to survive life that we forget to stop and assess whether our habits and lifestyles are pushing us closer to the life we want for ourselves. However, I've learned that at some point, we all have to face ourselves, take accountability, and come to Jesus.

I've had several come-to-Jesus moments throughout my life, and it's usually been before going to a higher level of faith. The first time I really sat in my truth was at the age of twenty-three after having an abortion. I made the decision to have an abortion after getting pregnant (by my now husband) during a very toxic point in our relationship. We were on the verge of breaking up, and I felt as though I only had two options. I could have the baby and end up a single mom of two kids or go to Iraq and make enough money to clear up my debt and get ahead financially. I often wish that someone in my circle would've tried to stop me from making one of the worst decisions of my life. Having that abortion sent me into a deep depression. Every time I tried to forget it, I thought about the way it felt having them literally suck the life out of me as if it was normal. I got off that table as a different woman. My relationship ended shortly after that, and I felt lost mentally, emotionally, and spiritually.

Still in shock about what happened a week prior, I started focusing on what made sense to me at the time. I thought to myself, if I could just get a degree and more money, I would never be in a position to need an abortion again. I headed to the Fort Hood Education Center to get registered for college. I thought I was going to sign up for classes, but I ended up having a run-in with Christ. I sat down with the education counselor and began telling him that I wanted to be a nurse, so I wouldn't have to be in the position of being abandoned, dependent, or broken again. Before I knew it, the tears started to flow so intensely that the counselor, with all of his prior experience, thought I had been raped. I was so ashamed and weighed down with the thought of it all that I couldn't hold it in anymore.

After calming down, I opened up to him and told him that I'd had an abortion. He paused and asked if I knew Jesus. I looked up and said, "Yes, Sir". He asked if I knew that Jesus had died for my sins, and again I said, "Yes, Sir". Things were all slowly starting to make sense. He then asked if I believed I could be forgiven for what I had done. It was at this question that a light bulb went off, and the weight was lifted as I slowly said for the third time, "Yes, Sir". He invited me to bible study, and I couldn't wait to get there. I had accepted Christ when I was young and went to church my entire life, but this was a moment of revival for me. God met me at the lowest point in my life and gave me hope again. After this moment, I just knew that it was time to separate myself from my old ways. I cried out, "God, I'm serious this time!"

To a certain extent, I meant it! I started cutting people off, I stopped clubbing, and I really gave living right my best effort. I can honestly say that changing the people, places, and things in my life made a huge impact. Everyone didn't understand it, but I knew if I was going to really walk with God, I had to change that stuff off top. I started going to church consistently, but in just a few months, Army duty called, and I was deployed to Iraq. We had a church out there, so I got active, and that made maintaining my confession to God much easier.

Like most of us humans do, I ended up falling back into some of my old ways, but this time it was different. It was like my spirit knew better, and because of that, I couldn't be as comfortable in my sin as before. As I continued to find my way while abroad, God was working some things out of me concerning men and "needing" to be with someone. When I look back, so many of my life struggles involved intimate relationships because I was always trying to find security, love, and validation in a man. I'm sure you can imagine the disappointment it often led to. Although my husband and I weren't together, I still really wanted to be with him. I talked to other dudes, but deep down, I was hoping and praying (basically begging, lol) for God to allow us to get back together even though things were no better between us. I just had a vision of us being together, and I was determined for it to happen no matter what. Because I hadn't done much work on myself, this soul tie just wouldn't let me move on completely. I'll talk more about that later...

However, when I made it home, I was determined to get back with him. It didn't happen immediately, but when it did, I tried my best to force him to marry me. I was ready, but he wasn't, which had been the case for all the previous years we were together. He came back to Texas, and we almost started the same cycle over again until my Pastor called me out. He stopped me in the hallway and asked me a question that really stuck with me. "When will you choose God over a man?". Bruh! First of all, I was mind-blown. Here was history repeating itself, and God had to bring me back to a place of decision. Either I was going to keep shacking and give up ministering, or my boyfriend could get his own place, and we could do it the right way. We agreed to have him get his own place, and within a couple of months, we ended up getting married. I was so happy to see how God worked it all out, but in reality, I played a big part in forcing my will instead of really waiting on God to do it organically.

About three years into my marriage, things were really bad. My self-esteem was at an all-time low, our finances weren't the best, and I was completely unhappy. I was working crazy hours as a basic training Drill Sergeant, and my husband and I were on two different pages. Girl, I don't even think we were in the same book. I had this vision of who I wanted him to be, and it was killing me that he wasn't where I "thought" he should have been spiritually. Instead of his spiritual development, he was more interested in motorcycle life. I would think to myself, "Bike life is going to destroy our marriage for sure because I did not sign up to be a biker's wife!". The more I complained, the more he pushed away. I'm sure my nagging made it even worse, but I believed I had to make sure he knew how I felt. Things got so bad that I honestly wanted to leave my marriage. The only thing that kept me holding on was the thought of my son growing up without a father the way I did. I knew that if we were going to make it, something was going to have to change. He had to change!

This brought me to another moment where God had to reveal Himself to me. This time, God showed me that if my husband was going to change, it would need to start with me. This was a hard pill to swallow because I felt justified in my behavior toward him. I knew I had a reason to nag, complain, have an attitude, not feel like having sex, and not ask for his input about family matters. Through my actions, I was telling him that I didn't need him, but in the same breath, I was mad because he wasn't finding his place in our family as the head of our home. As the saying goes, it was my way or the highway, but of course, I didn't really want him to hit the highway. I just wanted him to do what I said. I know, girl... it's giving Jezebel, but I could not see it at the time. I remember that there was an older lady in my life who told me how the Bible instructs us to get our husbands saved, and surprisingly, it didn't include me telling him how to be a man.

> *"Wives, in the same way, submit yourselves to your own husbands so that, if any of them do not believe the word, they may be won over without words but by the behavior of their wives." (1 Peter 3:1 NIV).*

This being the case, I had to face the awkward truth that I was going about my husband's salvation the wrong way. If he was supposed to be won over to Jesus by my behavior, it's safe to assume that he probably wanted nothing to do with God. I was a whole mess when I looked back. When I finally accepted what I needed to do, I had to ask God to help me. I had tried being nice, but it didn't last long because of all the resentment, anger, and disappointment I was feeling. I really tried to change, but it was clear that I could not change on my own. So there I was again... "Lord... I'm serious this time". I needed to change for the sake of saving my marriage!

I've found that one of the hardest parts about saving a marriage is that God doesn't change us or our spouses overnight. It feels hopeless at times, but we must have a mind that is set on the promises of God. Once our minds are set, we have to rely on our faith to keep us going when it seems like there is no progress. Faith is believing even when we don't see proof. It's viewing our negative reality as it really is, a bunch of lies from satan. If Satan can get us to give up prematurely, then he has met his objective. God honors covenant, and He doesn't give us a pass to divorce just because someone isn't maturing spiritually. If we keep it real, your husband probably does the same things you overlooked before getting married. A lot of times, the signs were there, but "love" was so powerful that we overlooked them. Remember, we all change and mature at different paces. Maybe you have grown, but his process may be different. As wives, we are obligated to love and pray for our husbands; however, we must admit that God has tried many times to help us avoid these struggles by encouraging us not to be unequally yoked in the first place. If you don't get yourself healed mentally, emotionally, and spiritually, you'll choose a man from a place of hurt, desperation, or a toxic understanding of love. I know you see the signs, so don't ignore them. There are still good men out here, but are you the good woman they are seeking? Who are you attracting? If it's clearly the wrong type of men, you may need to examine yourself to see WHY you are drawing men that are not healthy for you. It's time to let God mold you into that Proverbs 31 woman until He finds you. Now that I've gotten that out, back to how I got here, writing to you about getting serious with God.

The most recent time I got serious with God was for myself. I was caught up in doing so many things that I didn't have much time for God. Pouring into others, chasing military success, navigating entrepreneurship, keeping up with social media, conquering motherhood, and being a wife had me stretched thin. If a busybody was a person, it was me. I was doing all of these things with a pure motive, but something was still missing. I felt like I was checking things off a list with no clear direction from God. I wasn't hearing Him clearly, and I didn't like the burden of feeling that way. Because of the discomfort of this feeling, I felt led to start getting rid of some things. I came off social media, decided to stop the business, and started focusing more on my family and my relationship with God. It wasn't until I took time to pause that I realized how much I was missing out on with my oldest son. I realized that I was so focused on striving that I missed an opportunity to invest quality time into really getting to know my own son. He needed more of my attention, and I actually had time to give it to him.

Isn't that the enemy's objective, though? He gets us so caught up in our own ambitions, and it often leaves our children open to his attacks. They could be struggling with porn, self-esteem issues, learning challenges, sexuality, or fitting in, and we don't even notice because we are BUSY. Thank God that I realized when I did that, it was time to hit God up again..."Lord, I'm serious this time". I began to pray for God to help me prioritize what was really important. I prayed for God to help me let go of my selfish ambitions and do what mattered most. I prayed for God to change my desires and to help me be more loving and discerning. I prayed to God to help me train up my boys in a way that would bring Him Glory. I desired for God to pour into me, as I poured into them.

Then, above all, I prayed for God to give me the grace to do His will, which leads me here to you.

Now, it's your turn. It's time to sit with yourself and reflect on how you got to this very moment in life. What has led you to a place of wanting to get serious with God? What are you tired of repeating? What are you tired of striving for? Who are you tired of trying to impress or prove yourself to? Most importantly, what do you need from God? Keep in mind that 1 Peter 5:7 says, "casting all your cares [all your anxieties, all your worries, and all your concerns, once and for all] on Him, for He cares about you [with deepest affection, and watches over you very carefully]" (Amplified). He doesn't want you trying to do this life thing alone. Take it from me... You need help, Sis! Not from me, your sister, or your parents, but from God. Let Him help you, girl. Take this time to reflect and be real with God about how you got here. He already knows and is just waiting for you to acknowledge it so that the real change can start to take place.

Now, about you...

Where are you, and how did you get here? Assess where you are and the actions, mindsets, or values (or the lack of them) that got you here. List the good and the bad.

_____

_____

_____

_____

_____

Can you pinpoint anything that you know needs to change? Why?

_____

_____

_____

_____

What happens if you don't change?

_____

_____

Whew... First of all, I'm proud of you for taking the time to be real with yourself and own your part in where you are. Keep in mind that no one has it perfectly figured out, no matter how good their highlight reel looks. We all should allow God to transform our minds at the pace that He sees fit. It's a process, and I'm here to help you kick-start it by sharing what has worked for me. So, take a deep breath and let the transformation begin.

Paul was trying to help us when he said, "Don't copy the behavior and customs of this world, but let God transform you into a new person by **changing the way you think**. Then you will learn to know God's will for you, which is good and pleasing and perfect" (Romans 12:2 NLT). This is so important because the way you think now is based on your values, beliefs, what you saw growing up, things you've read, and people you trusted to lead you. We all grew up being influenced by culture, music videos, TV shows, friends, our surroundings, and experiences. Now God wants to change all of that, but you still have to put in the work. You have to put yourself in a position to learn about Him. That means spending less time scrolling social media and more time praying, reading your Bible, going to church, and listening to sermons.

Once God starts showing you things about yourself, it should encourage you to learn more and more about Him. If you don't discipline yourself to get in the habit of seeking God, everything else will always seem more important, and that's exactly where the enemy wants you to be. He knows that if you don't get any new information in, you'll keep doing the same things you've done over the years. That's not what you want. That's why you're reading this book. You're tired of starting and stopping. You're over doing all the things and still not feeling fulfilled. You know God has a purpose for you, and you're tired of getting in your own way. Yes, girl, it stops today! You are about to get serious with God, today! If you want to be excited but feel like you've been here before, just remember you didn't have the right tools for success last time. This time you're not just talking about it, but you've made up your mind that you are ready to put in the work. Say this affirmation with me, "I am not the same woman I was yesterday. I'm a whole new person! I'm intentional about healing, growing, and becoming the woman God intended for me to be!"

Let's Pray.

Lord,

Thank you for your grace over the years. Thank you for protecting me when I didn't even know I needed protection. Thank you for allowing me to make it to this moment in my life. Thank you for loving me when I didn't know how to love myself. Thank you for giving me another chance to tap into all that you have in store for me. Forgive me for the things I have done that didn't please you. Help me to recognize when I'm falling back into old mindsets, behaviors, and attitudes that will not get me the results I want in life. Show me what it means to live holy. Transform my mind. Show me the things you want me to change, and give me a desire to change them. Help me to get to know you, God. Take away any resentment or disappointments that may stop me from receiving your love. Help me to forgive others and myself the way you continue to forgive me. Help me to be a better person, Lord.

In Jesus' Name, Amen!

Chapter 2

Self-Sabotage... Am I Doing This to Myself?

"The reason that I can't find the enemy is that I have yet to look within myself."
– **Craig D. Lounsbrough**

"Self-sabotage is when we say we want something and then go about making sure it doesn't happen."
– **Alyce Cornyn-Sel**

Do you ever wonder why things just don't seem to go right in your life? I have found that many of the struggles we face are self-inflicted. Although we may not always intend to make our lives hard, sometimes it's done out of habit. So, before we start going deeper into how God wants to change our lives, we need to deal with **ourselves**.

More than likely, you trust yourself. When you hear your internal voice speaking to you, it usually sounds trustworthy. So, if you have a habit of talking negatively to yourself, the probability of you believing the negative talk is high. Many times, we've been misled to believe that, surely, we wouldn't say anything to harm ourselves. Wrong! Sometimes, we can be our worst critic and enemy. Sorry to say this, but you can't be trusted, Sis... at least not yet. On one side of the coin, we sometimes show grace and kindness to everyone except ourselves. Then, on the other side of the coin, at times, we can give ourselves too much grace as we are slow to stick to the disciplines that we know are going to move us forward. For example, you can convince yourself that a man loves you when you know he's only there to get one thing. You'll tell yourself you're really healed or unbothered by past trauma, but deep down, you're still affected. The comforting lies we tell ourselves are often the breeding ground for self-sabotage and prevent us from truly healing. The bottom line is that we need to be aware of when we are starting to self-sabotage.

I'm not excluded from this, Sis. If I'm not careful either, I'll convince myself of the very same lies. No matter how long one has been walking with Christ, there will always be opportunities to fall. In the past, I found myself knowing what was right, but still choosing wrong in the heat of the moment. Girl, I even premeditated a lot of the things that I did outside of the will of God. I've heard God and myself saying, "Girl, don't do that," and ignored us both, only to end up in regret. Luckily, God has the power to keep us from falling and the power to help us get back up if we already have. Because of God's goodness, He gives us the power to get up and experience His restorative grace, but only when we've really had enough.

Self-sabotage often finds its way into our lives because of a lack of preparation. If we say we want to get closer to God but don't discipline ourselves to study, pray, and fast, how can we expect to grow? We say we want to be healthier, but we skip the gym and choose the Crumbl cookies over the salad. We say we want men to take us seriously, but after a few weeks of dating, we are giving up the goods. We say we want to improve our credit, but we keep swiping for things we could do without. Doing nothing will sabotage you, Sis. So let's be real... have you been doing NOTHING? Have you been going through life with no vision or plan for your future? Are you full of plans but no action? Do you quit every time you start something because you lack discipline? Is where you are a result of your lack of intention?

Another way we self-sabotage is by allowing other people to mishandle us. As women, we often have a bad tendency to let those around us dump all their drama, negative energy, and self-inflicted problems on us without demanding that they take ownership. Basically, I'm saying that where there are no boundaries, self-sabotage flourishes. Now, there's a difference between supporting friends through rough seasons and upholding someone who is content with dysfunction. I remember times when my own friends had to establish boundaries with me because I didn't want any advice or wise counsel. I wanted to dump, but had no desire to hear the truth or any suggestions about what I was going through. In hindsight, I'm grateful that they stood firm on their boundaries because it made me aware that some things in my life desperately needed to change. I was messy, and my life was a direct reflection of all the trashy decisions I was making. All of that to say, sometimes we are called to be a source of light for our friends, and sometimes we have to guard our hearts and let them realize they are contributing to their own problems.

Self-Sabotage in Parenting

If we're not mindful, self-sabotage can lead us to repeating the things that we despised our parents for doing when we were young. We slowly forget how it felt to be misunderstood and ignored, and we fall into the cycles we were once a part of when raising our own children. We often vow to have a better relationship with them, not realizing that breaking cycles will require us to work through uncomfortable situations instead of blowing up or shutting down. Building a healthy relationship with our children requires us to deal with our attitudes, our patience, and our anger. If we blow up or shut down when something doesn't go our way, our children will eventually stop trying to trust us or open up to us.

Rest assured, I am speaking from personal experience. My frustration and approach to conflict once hindered my relationship with my son and caused me to spend a lot of time talking to him instead of listening. I didn't ask how he felt about situations that we were going through or how they affected him. It took me a while to recognize and accept that much of the frustration with my son came from a lack of thoughtful parenting and self-examination on my part. I wasn't intentional about helping him develop good habits for cleanliness and studying, but I was furious when he didn't keep his room clean and earn high grades. I had to get real with myself and decide to break the cycle of parental self-sabotage. All of a sudden, it hit me. He wasn't a grown man, and I hadn't taken the time to teach him the things I was frustrated about. Not only that, sometimes I wasn't demonstrating to him the skills I was expecting of him through my own actions. I was frustrated because his room wasn't clean, yet neither was mine. I was concerned about his low grades, yet I was satisfied with earning C's in my own studies. I was not considering my role in the things taking place in my life as a parent.

This form of self-sabotage not only affects our personal well-being but also impacts the well-being of our children. If we don't learn to call out our own self-sabotage and adjust accordingly, we will lose the opportunity to foster the healthy relationships we desire with our children. We must grow to ask ourselves, What is the true cost if the cycle continues? What if our children are learning to parent and live by observing us? Would we be proud of the outcome? We must examine the unconscious messages we are sending our children through the way we live our lives to be sure we are not setting them up to live lives filled with their own versions of self-sabotage.

I am not writing this section on self-sabotage in parenting to make you feel like a horrible parent, but it is my desire that you are aware of behaviors that can be shifted to change the dynamic of your relationships with your children. You may have messed some things up, but you are not too far gone; you can make those things right, starting right now. Think of ways you can be more kind, more patient, and more understanding with your kids. They may be resistant, but they will eventually learn to accept your new way of doing things. It's okay to be honest with your children about where you messed up. I wanted my son to know that I got it wrong so he wouldn't think my actions were normal. Taking accountability and improving the parent-child relationship will give you more access to influence their decisions and behavior. Girl, it's deep, and I plan to write a whole book on this topic as well, so for now, we'll keep it at the surface level.

Overcoming self-sabotage in parenting is fixing your part in the relationship. As you allow God to transform your mind with a new parenting normal, you will begin parenting differently. We must take responsibility for our roles in the lives of children and make things right. Remember that our default parenting style is often developed from what we saw growing up, our personalities (good or bad), and our visions of the role we play in our children's lives. How do you want them to remember you? What will they say they learned from watching and listening to you? When we take the time to think about the values, character, and skills we want our children to have, we then are able to effectively shift our approach to parenting, ridding it of self-sabotage. It won't always be easy, and at times you will mess up, but with patience, effort, and prayer, you can do it!

Self-Sabotage in Intimate Relationships

How was your relationship with your parents growing up? Were they present? Did they show you love and validate you? Did they make you feel valued and special? Or did they abandon you? Did they fail to protect you? Keep in mind a parent can be physically present but mentally and emotionally absent. In a sermon called "Glory Triggers," Minister and New York Times best-selling Author Sarah Jakes Roberts talked about triggers being an indication that we may still need healing, and I believe that's so true. My intention in mentioning this sermon is to push us to identify areas in our pasts that may still need healing so that we can stop sabotaging our present intimate relationships. Parental trauma often ranks high on many people's list when we begin to analyze how we navigate relationships with men (and God). Our relationship with our earthly parents often sets the tone for what we think love is. If we have to beg our parents for love, it will feel like second nature to beg someone for love. If you grew up trying to prove to your parents that you were worthy of their love, it will feel like second nature going out of your way physically, emotionally, and financially to prove your love. If you didn't feel loved by your parents at all, you can easily find yourself in a relationship with someone who doesn't love you at all while growing content, simply because you love them.

When my mother and father divorced, all of my siblings and I felt abandoned. I found myself doing all of the things I mentioned above because it felt like normal love to me. I had no idea what love was, so I accepted anything that felt right to me. I didn't like how I felt after giving myself to men that didn't value me, but my lack of knowledge had me repeating toxic cycles mindlessly. I thought that I could prove myself worthy by attempting to change the men I found myself dating, hoping he would soon recognize my value. The truth is, we all just want to be loved, but we often go about finding and maintaining love the wrong way. Knowing what true love is will help you more readily recognize the counterfeit.

God says that "Love is patient and kind. Love is not jealous or boastful or proud or rude. It does not demand its own way. It is not irritable, and it keeps no record of being wronged. It does not rejoice about injustice but rejoices whenever the truth wins out. Love never gives up, never loses faith, is always hopeful, and endures through every circumstance" (1 Corinthians 13:4-7 NLT). This is how God loves us, and as we get closer to Him, we become more aware of all of the times he's been patient, kind, and forgiving when humans sometimes were not. As we learn to receive this love from our Heavenly Father, we are able to extend that same love to ourselves. When we learn to be patient, kind, and forgiving to ourselves, we are then able to extend scriptural love to others and accept it from others. I am sure that sometimes good men have tried to love us, but because we didn't understand real love, we often pushed it away. It's time for us to shift our view of our love for God, ourselves, and others so that we are better prepared to receive love in return without the stain of self-sabotage.

Now, while God wants us to love people this way, he tells us to be careful about falling in love with someone who does not share our values and beliefs. You've probably heard the scripture, "Do not be yoked together with unbelievers. For what do righteousness and wickedness have in common? Or what fellowship can light have with darkness?" (1 Corinthians 6:14 NIV). This scripture was referring to all relationships, both platonic and intimate. Many times when we are not intentional about our faith, an unbeliever will seem like a good match because we are not found where we need to be spiritually. Sure, he looks like a man of God, but that's because we have not been found in the word enough to recognize the good from the godly. We often haven't allowed God to transform our minds, so we fall into the habit of choosing based on preferences. We let height, build, complexion, job status, and charisma draw us in before considering his character, goals, work ethic, leadership abilities, and genuine concern for you. I'm just saying that sometimes we sabotage ourselves because we have not done the internal work on ourselves to attract and maintain the right type of man. We'll talk more about becoming the Proverb 31 woman in a later chapter.

Recognizing self-sabotage doesn't end in the dating stage; we also have to be careful not to let it creep into our established intimate relationships. I remember several years into my marriage when I realized abandonment was showing up in our arguments. Whenever my husband and I argued, I feared it would lead to him leaving. In my mind and body, I felt overwhelmed with anger, fear, sadness, and the need to prove myself right so he would stay. After my husband learned of my abandonment trigger, he assured me, saying, "When I'm arguing with you, I'm not thinking about leaving, I just don't agree". Girl, in my mind, disagreement meant separation was coming soon. When you're angry, fearful, and emotional, it's very hard to communicate and very easy to self-sabotage. I hope you can see how I was self-sabotaging here and know that I want better for you and your relationships.

Women often self-sabotage out of fear. Fear of being alone sometimes causes us to lower our standards in our relationships. Deep down, we start to feel like we're not enough to keep a man interested, at least without the aspect of sex. I've been there, sis. This is often because we haven't realized our true value. Fear also has a way of hindering us from believing that a man can genuinely love us without hidden motives. The pain and trauma of love with motives can feel so real that we find it hard to unmask and be vulnerable afterward, leading to questioning everything. I understand this firsthand and have come to realize that, in most cases, we can look back and see all the signs that told us not to enter the relationships that hurt us in the past. The more we mature, the more we're able to see glaring red flags that the past version of ourselves couldn't see at the time.

However, we must be careful not to sabotage our future relationships because of past trauma or lack of insight from those of the past. We often claim we're ready for the "right" man to come along, but if we're mentally, spiritually, and emotionally stagnant, we'll repeat the same cycle. No, you may not fall for the exact same red flags, but you'll choose a man based on a shallow understanding of what you want. The more you get to know yourself, the more you'll know who is and isn't right for you, and the less likely you are to self-sabotage receiving love from those who are. If we don't know who we are, how can we possibly determine the man that is right for us?

Also, keep in mind that God knows all of our potential and sees us operating as our best selves. The man he has in store for you will complement that version of you. When we choose to enter into intimate relationships without doing the internal work on ourselves, we'll probably struggle in the process. All I'm saying is that we cannot risk self-sabotaging our relationships by neglecting to improve ourselves first. If you are single, take your single season to get close to God. He will lead and guide you if you're close to Him, living His word, and listening to Him. Trust me, choosing a man in your own wisdom will lead to unnecessary struggles. It's time to stop getting this part wrong and do it God's way. There are godly men who want to love the daughters of God, but we have to first prepare ourselves to identify, receive, and give the right type of love in return.

Self-Sabotage in Your Career

Why have you labeled the career of your dreams as impossible? What stops you from applying for the promotion? Why is it hard to envision yourself doing what you love every day? Do you even know what you would love to do every day, or have you been so busy working that you haven't had time to think about what would make you feel fulfilled? When did you let life tell you to give up on being YOUR version of successful? Do you feel stuck in a job or career that doesn't seem to be going anywhere? If you struggled to answer any of these questions, it's probably because you lack clarity about what you really want, and you have fallen into the traps of self-sabotage.

The reason I put this topic in the self-sabotage chapter is because there is only one person who can determine what you desire in a career: YOU. When we don't get to know ourselves or develop a plan for our futures, we end up stuck and in cycles of hopelessness. Sis, it is time for us to stop just going through the motions. Our awareness of the lack of fulfillment in our lives often becomes self-sabotage when we don't make an effort to change the narrative. We must realize that where we are in our respective careers right now is because of how we did or did not plan, take action, or have a vision for ourselves.

Before reading self-help books, having a vision for my life seemed like something only teenagers would do. My whole life started to change as I embraced thinking about seeing myself live a certain way every day. Even now, when I speak of what I desire to do after my time in the military, people think it's a little far-fetched. This far-fetched vision has led me to take action over the past seven years and has placed me on a track to be exactly where I want to be when I retire. It started with a vision. Call me crazy, but I literally envision myself getting up every morning, getting the kids off to school, working out, having my cup of coffee while working my online business, and being paid thousands for speaking at schools and organizations about leadership and ethics. I can't simply stay at the place of vision, though. Vision must be paired with a plan. I know that if I want this to become a reality, I have to plan backward. This means thinking about everything it will require to make my vision a reality for me. I've found that the shift from vision to plan is where self-sabotage manifests for most people.

We often have the vision but no plan for how we will make it a reality. Sis, after we get the vision, we have to break that thing down into actionable steps. What will it really take to get there? Will it take a degree, start-up costs, mentorship, new friends, forgiveness, more time with God, more exercise, less eating, or more discipline? Decide on a few things you can do in a year to get closer to the outcome you want. Then, decide what needs to happen every month, week, and day. I'm telling you now, Sis, if you don't take these steps for your career or business, it will remain a dream. If you have the vision, it's time to take action! No more excuses, and being disappointed when the new year rolls around and you're in the same spot as the previous year. Don't allow your dream to die!! You're not too young or too old to flourish, you're just not disciplined and bold enough to go for your heart's desires. Maybe you haven't taken time to write the strategy because you thought it would just happen without your input and effort. No, Ma'am! It's time to get intentional, serious, bold, and disciplined!

I encourage you to use this space below to write a vision for your life. Don't be limited by anything in your current circumstances. With God, all challenges can be overcome when we seek Him and allow Him to put us in alignment with His will. Be warned that the enemy will try to tell you that this process is pointless, and even make you feel silly for doing it. However, there's a scripture that says, "Where there is no vision [no revelation of God and His word], the people are unrestrained" (Proverbs 29:18 AMP). This means that when we don't know God's word, we will do whatever *feels* good at the moment, and we won't have the discipline to stay focused on achieving the things God has placed on our hearts.

What's amazing is that the first vision I had for my life was naturally focused on me and my own ambitions and dreams. Over time, He has shifted my vision to align with His Word. I always wanted to use my story and experiences to help teen girls and women, but now it's more in line with the scripture that says, "These older women must train the younger women to love their husbands and their children, to live wisely and be pure, to work in their homes, to do good, and to be submissive to their husbands. Then they will not bring shame on the word of God" (Titus 2:3-5). That's it, that's one of my desires and goals. I didn't know it then, but God has changed my heart and mind to line up with His scriptures. Ultimately, God wants us to be happy serving Him. Thus, writing a vision gives you a chance to share with Him your ideas and desires so that He can start to shape and mold you into the person He created you to be. This vision may shift or change down the road, but for now, Write The Vision, and don't hold back. Also, for my sisters who find this a bit challenging, it's ok. Start small, and the more God shows you who you are, the more clear your purpose will become. You can start with things like the following:

- I want to be a confident woman who does not need validation from others to feel good.

- I want to be a good mother who is patient, understanding, and loving so that my kids will trust me.

- I want to be a healthy person internally and externally by having a healthy lifestyle.

- I want to be myself regardless of who I am around, I don't want to change for people.

- I want to stop letting people take advantage of me and have boundaries with those I love.

- I want to take vacations without worrying about how I will pay bills afterward.

- I want to be confident in my purpose, and please God with my life.

- I want to wake up every morning and have the freedom to work wherever I want.

As you can see, your vision can be material and spiritual. I think it's important to consider the person you want to become internally so that you can push yourself to achieve the external vision. Make it personal and meaningful so that you'll want to stay committed to becoming this version of yourself. In the future, you'll be able to look back at your vision to see if you are coming into alignment with the things you envisioned for yourself. If you find yourself becoming the total opposite, it will be a gentle reminder to adjust your thinking and actions.

Take the space below to think forward. It is not about who you are now or who you were back then, but about the woman you want to become. Who are you as your highest self? Considering all we've just talked about, write a vision for who you want to become.

I want to become a woman that...

_____

_____

_____

_____

_____

Let's reflect... What are some ways you self-sabotage? How have you been contributing to not accomplishing your goals?

_____

_____

_____

_____

Write one goal you must achieve to become your highest self.

_____

_____

_____

_____

What is one thing you need to change in your daily lifestyle to start moving closer to your highest self?

_____

_____

_____

_____

What usually stops you from achieving your goal (this one in particular, if you have tried it before)?

How can you avoid this pitfall again? (Example: meal prepping if eating out ruins your diet)

Let's Pray.

Lord, forgive me for standing in my own way at times. Forgive me for doing things my way and for not allowing You to be the ultimate guide in my life. Thank you for showing me the ways that I need to allow Your word to change my mind and my thought process. Thank you for showing me that I'm capable of thinking and acting differently. Thank you for making me unique, and help me to accept that my life should not look like anyone else's. Help me to develop a vision for my life that aligns with Your will and purpose for me. I know the plans You have for me are good and not evil, and will give me hope for the future (Jeremiah 29:11). Help me to trust that You know best, even when it may not feel good. Change my desires if they are not in line with Your plan for my life. Lord, help me to forgive myself and others for past decisions that brought me hurt and pain. Help me give my younger self grace for only doing what she knew to do. Help me to become the best version of myself. I will no longer self-sabotage. I will no longer stand in my own way. I will learn, grow, be gentle with myself, and most importantly rely on You to guide me. Thank you for loving me as I am right now, and calling me higher because you know that I'm capable. I can do all things through Christ who strengthens me. Strengthen me right now, Lord!

In Jesus' Name, Amen!

Chapter 3

Shaped by the "Culture"

Do not conform to the pattern of this world, but be transformed by the renewing of your mind. Then you will be able to test and approve what God's will is—his good, pleasing and perfect will.

(Romans 12:2)

Have you ever wondered how someone could grow up in a home with great Christian parents, a city with low crime rates, and great role models, but somehow still become the opposite of their upbringing? Umm hmm, CULTURE! Culture is defined as socially transmitted behavior and ways of thinking. It includes the norms found in society, as well as the knowledge, beliefs, arts, laws, customs, and habits of the individuals in a group. The presence of culture means that you can teach your child certain values and beliefs, but schools, friends, television, laws, and influencers have the ability to convince them another way is better. For example, most of our moms told us not to have sex because we could get pregnant or contract an STD. We gave our best effort to listen at first, but then we were bombarded with music videos, TV shows, and fellow fourteen-year-old friends who convinced us that the pleasure was worth the risk. Think back to what the people you looked up to were doing and promoting? Culture is powerful when you are not firm on who you are and what you stand for. If you pay attention to the common themes you see on television shows, news, radio, and within new laws, you'll get an idea of the essence of American culture.

When you think about the American culture of womanhood, what kind of mindset, behavior, and character do most songs, television shows, and major influencers encourage us to have? One common theme is being over-sexualized and the promotion of promiscuity (a casual or undiscriminating approach to sex). We see these themes in all of the movies, TV shows, and social media profiles of those that seem to be living their best lives. Worldly female songwriters and rappers seem to celebrate and promote being the side chick, not needing or wanting a man, and having sex with no strings attached. Sza's song *The Weekend* bragged about keeping someone else's man satisfied on the weekend and sending him back home to his girlfriend. Listen, the beat was fire, but the lyrics had women subconsciously excited about being the other woman.

I don't know if you've been the other woman before, but honestly, it's nothing to be proud of. First, he's basically saying you are not worthy of his undivided commitment. Secondly, you're hurting another woman and lowering your self-worth. Whew, girl, that's a lot to unpack, but what gets us to that point in real life? Desperation, low self-esteem, low self-worth, an incorrect understanding of love, and repeatedly choosing the wrong type of man are what gets us to these low places. Since I'm being honest, that was the case for me the one time I entertained someone else's husband. Listening to songs that encourage and agree with our sin and negative feelings encourage us to find contentment in those situations, instead of feeling convicted to change. Through Sza's lyrics, she was influencing millions of women and girls to take on a toxic mindset by normalizing her low self-esteem and desperation on top of a nice beat. I get it, because this aspect of culture influenced me too earlier in life.

There was a song called *In My Mind by* Heather Headley that came out the year I graduated high school in 2006. In this song, she was saying that even though her relationship ended, she would remain his girlfriend in her mind. Makes no sense right? Later, I would intentionally listen to that song when I split with my husband, knowing that I desperately wanted him back (before we were married). It would have me emotional, and eventually calling to see if he felt the same. Ultimately, I ended up looking desperate and emotionally attached in an unhealthy way. Meanwhile, he was listening to music telling him to move on to the next woman. Now that I understand the power of music, I know that it doesn't always encourage logical thinking. Most of the time music plays into our emotions, and then those emotions flow into our decision making when faced with real-life decisions. Hear me, Sis, culture has a sneaky way of making its way to our souls.

    Honestly, I went through a wild season after high school, and I was not proud of the woman I had become. Deep down, I knew better than my behavior displayed, but I was convinced I would find love the way the culture said I would, by degrading my body and compromising my spirit. I had it all wrong. I only ended up feeling used, let down, and worthless because I only saw myself as valuable if I was someone's woman. Even though I had gone to church my whole life, no one had ever taught me how valuable I was to God and how sex, relationships, and material things could never validate me the way God does. As God's word transformed my mind, I became more confident in my value. That confidence did not come because of my looks, achievements, or sexual abilities, but because I was learning a new form of value, a value that was internal. My mind and my character were slowly changing, but the process would have never started if I was continuously being influenced by the culture. I had to start letting the ways of the culture go, including the music.

How the Devil Shapes Culture and You

God warns us not to conform to the patterns of this world for good reason. The crazy thing is that our flesh (our natural body and mind without the Holy Spirit's guidance) naturally wants to do just that. If we are not careful, we will allow the music, lifestyles, and attitudes of the world to become normal to us. Not only that, we will start to enjoy and desire the shallow and sinful things of the world, just as the world does. When I mention *"The world", I am referring to the* people who do not belong to the Kingdom of God. People who have no intention of being guided by God's principles usually live their lives doing whatever feels good to them at the moment without ever considering God. Satan uses music to encourage sex, promiscuity, drugs, toxic relationships, and things that lower your self-worth. All of these things are designed to distract us from the true purpose God has for our lives. Think about it, God is going to have a difficult time getting through to a person who is always high, drunk, in a toxic relationship, or distracted by things that have no real value. Those who spend all day watching their favorite TV show (with no added value to their life) and only five minutes reading their Bible, won't see much change in their minds. Those who get their ideas about womanhood, life, and sex from what they see and hear in culture are bound to have trouble.

Listening to one nasty song probably won't have us living crazy lifestyles, but listening to a progressively promiscuous genre of music over time (which most of us have) is going to have an impact on the way we think. If nothing else, it has the potential to desensitize us to certain behaviors. I know for certain that I used to sing many gangster rap songs that encouraged a lifestyle I wanted nothing to do with. I was rapping about smoking weed and killing people simply because the beat was good. I have never agreed with either of those things, but somehow singing about them made me feel a sense of belonging when I knew every word to Lil' Boosie's *Set It Off* song. Guess what? Even though I haven't heard the song in years, I still know every word. Meanwhile, learning scriptures that will transform my mind in a positive way is challenging at times. When we embrace these lyrics and the behaviors they promote, we begin to default to them when we don't have other values in place to counteract bad values. Without realizing it, I was allowing Satan's puppets to shape my mind.

What has been shaping your mind all these years? Are your standards, self-esteem, and thought processes shaped by people you admire or God's word? Our values give us boundaries. There are some who never had any values other than those they've seen and heard about from unreliable sources. God's word gives us values and principles to live by, but we have to make them a part of who we are. For example, God tells us in His Word to wait until marriage to have sex, yet everything in culture says the exact opposite. However, you will think twice about casual sex when you learn the value of being someone's wife in the future. You'll understand that giving it up so easily, as the culture suggests, will potentially cloud your judgment when making important decisions.

> *"If then you have been raised with Christ, seek the things that are above, where Christ is, seated at the right hand of God. 2 Set your minds on things that are above, not on things that are on earth".* **Colossians 3:1-2 *(ESV)***

In the above scripture, we see that God tells us to do the exact opposite of what our flesh wants and Satan endlessly recommends. The enemy wants us to get caught up in striving for material and temporary happiness. God, on the other hand, tells us to set our minds on eternal things that please Him. When our minds are set on pleasing God, some things become non-negotiable. Sure, our flesh may feel tempted to smoke weed, get drunk, use horoscopes, and engage in that toxic yet physically satisfying relationship, but is that really what God wants for us? When I was living in sin, I didn't know or care what the Bible expected of me, but I could always still sense I was doing something wrong. Naturally, after doing something repetitively, we numb ourselves to the negative feelings that initially came with the act, but deep down our consciences cry out for us to do better. The Holy Spirit wants better for us. The Devil loves when everything around us encourages us to keep living in sin. He loves when we choose to stay in a depressing situation. He loves when we keep living an unhealthy lifestyle because he knows that he doesn't have to do much work for your destruction. A life without holy boundaries and limitations will give us instant gratification, but there is no long-term reward.

Think about it, anything worth having requires sacrifice. Having a good marriage, raising good children, having good health, and being financially stable all require some sort of sacrifice. The entire premise of us having access to salvation began with a sacrifice. Jesus knew that we would find ways to mess up our lives, so He wanted us to have a way to be forgiven for our intentional and unintentional errors. God knew that just like Eve, we would be tempted and at times give in to temptation. The devil is banking on us staying just the way we are. He is okay with us working, paying our bills, and consuming so much Facebook content that we never take time to pick up our Bibles and discover our purpose. This level of distraction happens to the majority of people, but we are not the majority anymore. I know deep down that we realize how culture has shaped who we were in the past, but now we should want God to shape and mold us into the women He intended for us to be. Yes, we are going to be tempted; we must earnestly ask God to change our desires. We must ask Him to help us live in this world without doing what the world does.

The "Do What You Want" Mentality

Can you imagine your child or younger sibling deciding to do whatever they wanted regardless of the rules they have been given? Can you imagine a world where everyone ignored laws and did whatever they wanted? Even though these boundaries are given for protection, what if those around you were only concerned about what makes them feel good in the moment? This example is similar to how God views us disobeying His principles and doing things our own way. We often don't care about the protection that comes with obedience because we want to do what WE want instead. Today, we have glamorized the attitude of independence. Eve set us all up for failure when she chose to be independent and do what she wanted instead of what God said. After listening to Satan, Eve ate the fruit, even though she knew God instructed her not to do so.

> *4 Then the serpent said to the woman, "You will not surely die. 5 For God knows that on the day you eat of it your eyes will be opened, and you will be like God, knowing good and evil." 6 So when the woman saw that the tree was good for food, that it was pleasant to the eyes, and a tree desirable to make one wise, she took of its fruit and ate.* **Genesis 3: 4-6 (NKJV).**

First, we see that Eve allowed the Serpent (the father of lies) to convince her that God was a liar. He's still doing that to many people today. Satan attempts to convince us that God is holding us back from fun, pleasure, success, and freedom by giving us boundaries and commandments when, in reality, he's actually protecting us. Satan makes sex, drugs, laziness, toxic relationships, procrastination, and fear feel like a better option than God. In reality, following Satan's lead only leads to the destruction and death of our purpose. Eve also got distracted by what she saw with her eyes. How many times have we done that? How many times have we just disregarded God's guidance (knowingly or unknowingly) and chosen to make a decision based on what looks good to our eyes? We may give up on a goal because we don't see the results we want. We may end our marriages because we don't see the possibility of our husbands changing. The sight of your child's out-of-control behavior might make you want to give up on them instead of showing them loving kindness. Instead of doing it God's way, some of us may give up on being abstinent because we meet a man who is showing husband potential.

Faith requires us to do what God wants of us, even when we don't see what we want to see. It also requires us to trust His way, even when what we want is looking us in the face like the fruit was for Eve. I'm telling you, the enemy is still deceiving many of us today with the same tactics. He loves when we become so prideful that we don't consider God's will for us. As we continue living lives that are distracted from God's will, doing our own thing becomes a normal way of life. Eve's one act of disobedience had major consequences, as have some of the decisions we've made in the past. Can you think back to one decision you made that would have ended differently had you consulted God? Trust me, I know this firsthand.

When most Christians think of satanism (devil worshipers), they imagine the red monster with horns, or people with black fingernails, hair, and clothes. This image has been pushed with great intention to make us think of Satan as a fictional character. Meanwhile, Satanists actually believe in being their own self-god. Many of them look just like you, but live by the motto "Do as thou wilt". Yes, do whatever you want. Satanists believe in a lifestyle with no boundaries, limits, or accountability. Can you imagine how dangerous our world would be if Aleister Crowley, infamous English occultist, convinced millions of people to think and behave according to satanist ideals? Guess what? So many Christians are already supporting this agenda that is in complete opposition to God's will. This is why God tells us to deny ourselves, because He knows just how reckless we can be if left to our own desires and rationale. Contrary to the philosophy of satanism, we really do need boundaries and principles to live by if we want to get the most out of this life. God gives us the freedom to choose whether we want to live within those boundaries, but to be clear, living outside of them comes with a cost.

When I first realized I needed to give up secular music, I was distraught. I had no clue what I was going to do without the music that I had lived my entire life relating to, loving, and learning life lessons from. Surely, I was convinced that life would not be the same (in a negative way). I couldn't imagine riding and working out to worship music for the rest of my life. Yeah, the music I loved was talking about killing people, dropping it like it was hot, and even taking pride in being whores, but I knew I would never really do any of those things. Or did I? With the right song on, I went from being a whore to a "Bad B****" within a few seconds. This type of behavior was exactly what He was warning me not to do, but because the beat was catchy, I let the message of the music slide right into my mind. My point here is that conforming to the world can sometimes be subtle. We don't have to be living a total rockstar lifestyle to be considered conformists. With every little compromise, we allow the culture to shape the way we view sin and become desensitized to the things God wants us to steer far away from. God doesn't recommend not conforming to make our lives boring, but He does so because He knows that even subtle mindset shifts will hinder us from striving to live Holy. Maybe we're not actually killing people (thank God for that) by way of the music we listen to, but we also are not allowing God to truly cleanse us from all unrighteousness so that we can be set apart. God wants a clear distinction between people who live in the world and those who live in the Kingdom of God. Sure, we go to church and visit the kingdom weekly, but do the lifestyles that we live on Monday through Saturday conform more to the world or the kingdom of God?

Ms. INDEPENDENT

The world has led us to believe that being independent should be our ultimate goal as women. Let's be clear, I'm not saying that we should go into womanhood without ambitions as we look for a man to "take care of us", but being submitted and provided for shouldn't be seen as a weakness either. I just want to present the thought that sometimes, being too independent can hinder us from allowing a man to assume his role as a leader in our lives. I'll get much deeper later, but for now, let me tell you how I started my Ms. Independent journey.

I know that this subject is a little sensitive, but I'm gonna touch on it anyway. Lil' Webbie lied to us! I remember first hearing the 2007 anthem, I.N.D.E.P.E.N.D.E.N.T, and feeling a couple of ways. The first way that I felt was empowered. As a fresh high school graduate, independence meant uncommon freedom, and I couldn't wait to experience it. My mother refused to let me live my "best life" under her roof, so once I finished high school, it was time to go get my own roof. I thought that getting my own house, car, two jobs, and becoming a bad broad was right within reach.

Wrong! Little did I know, all those things required money and resources that I didn't have access to at the time. I was singing the song, but I was far from independent.

The second thought I had was, "men want an independent woman, so if I'm going to attract a man, I need to be independent". I figured if Lil' Webbie (the epitome of manhood in my 18-year-old mind) wanted an independent woman, so did all the regular men. So, that became the goal. Basically, I thought that I would do what I had to do to become successful, and men would be lined up to love me. I assumed I had a leg up in the game because I already knew how to "prove my love to a man" from my complicated relationship with my father. I had already learned that if I was able to loan my father money, and pay his bills from time to time, I would receive his love and validation. This principle soon transferred to my way of thinking in my relationship dynamics with other men. Ding, Ding, Ding!! I was about to have it all! Success, a good man to take care of, and all the stress, pressure, and drama that came with it. So without realizing it, my mind was subconsciously set, and independence was the goal.

What the rappers didn't tell me was that this independence also came coupled with an attitude that most real men did not find attractive. We know this attitude in more modern terms as the "I want a man, but I don't need a man" mindset. I have found that most good men don't want anything to do with that attitude because their goal is to take care of and provide for their wives and family. God wired men that way. So, if the idea of "needing" a man makes you cringe, the way of the culture may have gotten to you. I know I'm stepping on some toes, but I just know that my toes were first run over by a car because I spent a lot of time thinking just like this, too. Who wants to be seen as weak and needy? Who wants to put all their trust in a man, only to be let down? Well, if it makes you feel any better, we have been culturally conditioned to be attracted to the wrong type of men. A man who doesn't want responsibility ultimately wants you to be responsible for him. Yeah, I see now that Lil' Webbie basically wanted someone to be his mama. Culture has continued to do a really good job at encouraging us to be insanely independent. It has lowered the value of marriage and upped the value of casual sex. If we're being honest, most of the behavior culture encourages makes us less desirable for marriage. It often forces us to be independent much longer than we'd like.

Most of the black women in films are portrayed as strong and capable of doing everything on their own. They don't seem to need a man, and they manage to be successful in doing it all. I can only recall a few shows that showed a black woman being properly loved and cared for by her husband. Instead, the single mother was often the hero, as she often is in reality due to absent fathers. But why is that? Why are 75% of African American homes without fathers today? Why does the black woman seem to enjoy working, paying all the bills, raising the kids, and playing the savior in most films and storylines? Why are there no good black fathers in mainstream movies? Why are we more consistently shown condoning music that degrades and sexualizes us more than other races? I don't have a clear memory of ever hearing one woman speak against how black women were being portrayed in hip-hop culture. Instead, "video vixens" influenced our expression because channels like BET showed black people thriving in those lifestyles.

Speaking of BET, once while visiting my in-laws, they had the BET awards playing in the background. I couldn't help but notice that the things that were awarded and congratulated were the very things that destroy black homes and communities. Black people were being rightfully praised for their musical giftedness; however, while many of them were succeeding on screen, their private lives were later exposed for being filled with sex, drugs, and alcohol addictions. Everything looked like fun, but I couldn't help but wonder if the fun was worth it? Our cultural icons often live and parade flagrant, money-filled, worldly lifestyles, never thinking about the effect on the everyday person who is following their lead.

As an audience of followers, we are left to deal with absent, drug-addicted, and imprisoned fathers who are trying to live out what they have heard in hip-hop music. Our girls are often convinced from a young age that their value lies in how many men they can attract and how good they can make a man feel sexually. Premarital sex is portrayed as freedom, as culture ignores the number of unwanted pregnancies that lead to fatherless children, and even abortion. Music that advances the hypersexual agenda also often leaves out the part about sexually transmitted diseases and feelings of emptiness after giving ourselves to someone who just wanted a good time. The devil is very strategic in his use of music and media because he knows that if we ignore our conscience around these things for the sake of a good beat, it will become natural to us.

I think it's much deeper than a woman's need for hyper-independence, though. This need for independence is often birthed from systematic origins. I believe the evolution of music from funk to gangster rap changed the culture in a way that most people don't realize. I am also convinced that Willie Lynch's method for *Breaking The Black Woman* has been modernized. Now, I'm sure you're thinking, "here we go with the "slave talk", but just go with me for a minute. I want to show you the escalation of fatherlessness in comparison to the music that was influencing black culture during past eras. First, let me show you where the strong black man's image was initially destroyed.

Let's take a look at how the family was structured in slavery. In the book *The Making of a Slave,* by Willie Lynch, the author explains how black men were often emasculated and nearly beaten to death in front of women and children. This form of humiliation left women feeling alone and unprotected, forcing them to be independent. Women were so afraid of their sons being treated the same way that they decided to be quiet and out of sight. Women were made to be leaders or protectors against their wills. With those circumstances, the need for independence is understandable, but I think we are still experiencing the effects of this psychological manipulation today. Below is an excerpt of Willie's guidance on how to break the black woman. Uncoincidentally, it's by breaking her reliance on the black man.

*We have reversed the relationship in her natural uncivilized state: she would have a strong dependency on the uncivilized n-word male, and she would have a limited protective tendency toward her independent male offspring and would raise male offspring to be dependent like her. Nature had provided for this type of balance. We reversed nature by burning and pulling a civilized n-word apart and bull whipping the other to the point of death, all in her presence. By her being left alone, unprotected, with the **male image destroyed**, the* *ordeal caused her to move from her psychological dependent state to a frozen independent state. In this frozen psychological state of independence, she will raise her **male** and female offspring in reversed roles. For **fear** of the young males life she will psychologically train him to be **mentally weak and dependent, but physically strong**. Because she has become psychologically independent, she will train her **female offsprings to be psychological independent**. What have you got? You've got the **n-word woman out front and the n-word man behind and scared**. This is a perfect situation of sound sleep and economy. (The Making of A Slave: Willie Lynch)*

If this strategy worked in slavery, it's very possible that the same modernized strategy can be effective today. Instead of the images displayed by Willie Lynch's vivid imagery, we now see black men being killed, caught drug dealing, being locked up, boasting about having kids out of wedlock, living homosexual lifestyles, and degrading women down to just objects for sexual pleasure. All of these things distract them from being present fathers and husbands. The distraction and absence of the man takes away the woman's ability to trust and need a man in the way God intended. I think a majority of this modern-day Wille Lynch conditioning has taken place through music. While music itself isn't physically harming or enslaving us, it is encouraging behavior that leads to physical and mental imprisonment. Consider the escalation of this psychological manipulation and influence through the different genres of music.

In the 1960's, fatherlessness was only around 19.9% in African American homes and 6.1% in white homes. The music in the 1960s wasn't as blatantly sexual as we know music to be today, but it definitely was the start of the letdown of the moral guard most people had back then. This was around the time that popular culture was introduced to mainstream funk music. James Brown, The Isley Brothers, Marva Whitney, and Bobby Womack were leading the way in music and paving the way for Hip-Hop. In the 1970s, the fatherlessness rate increased to 29.5% in black homes and 7.8% in white homes. In 1979, Sugar Hill Gang dropped *Rappers Delight*, which was the first hip hop song to play on the radio. I was born eight years later, and still know this infamous first line:

I said-a hip, hop, the hippie, the hippie

To the hip hip hop-a you don't stop the rock

It to the bang-bang boogie, say up jump the boogie

To the rhythm of the boogie, the beat

Harmless, right? Not really. From the surface, the song sounds innocent and like a good time. But, after reading all the lyrics and doing a little research, I see how it glorified the behavior that destroyed the black community during that era. The rappers talked about getting "spank," also known as cocaine, being the ladies' pimp, and busting women out with "super sperm." With the presence of a good beat, you may not think much of it, but with more examination, the subconscious message being broadcast to our communities was a little different. People were seeing images of successful black cocaine users, the over-sexualization of black women, and the start of engaging in sex with no intention of fathering the children that came out of it. Crazy, right? Yes, but this was just the beginning.

In 1980, fatherlessness increased to 43.9% in black homes and just 13.1% in white homes. Justice Department figures show that from 1990 to 2000, 50 percent of the growth in inmate populations at state prisons was for violent crimes, and that 20 percent was for drug crimes. With fewer fathers and role models in homes, more black men were being influenced by songs like "Straight Outta Compton" by Niggaz With Attitude (NWA), which was released in 1989 and quickly rose to the top of the charts. Girl, this song took the culture in a whole new direction. We were bragging about killing each other without getting caught, and people were loving it! Do you think that the increase in violence and drugs could have been influenced by the mainstream promotion of these things by people that look like us? If you read the lyrics, you'll get an idea of how common it was to disrespect women and how popular culture viewed men as suckers for loving women and taking care of their families. Music artists were offering their listeners a whole new set of values, and it clearly worked. But was this just a coincidence, or was this intentional?

Here is where I drop a little conspiracy. For years, rappers have been speaking out about private prisons being likened to modern-day slavery. Private prisons are filled with inmates who are paid pennies to build hundreds of items, which are then sold to businesses for profit. Rappers like Bizzy Bone and David Banner talk about how investors pay music labels millions of dollars to market crime, drugs, and sex to listeners in hopes of gaining more inmates. This is deep because most young boys try to imitate the lifestyles these rappers sing about and end up incarcerated. Did you know that although black men only account for 13% of the US population, they make up 35% of the incarcerated? I'm no mathematician, but the math ain't mathing. So, all I'm saying is that none of what popular culture offers benefits women or men in the African American community. If the culture has its way, women will continue to be forced into unrealistic independence due to a lack of strong, black, male leaders. We need more good men (not influenced by rap culture) so that women can feel safe being dependent again. Fatherlessness impacts us in many ways, and being aware of these deficits can help us seek healing and restoration in the areas that keep us in counterproductive cycles. I need you to know that God doesn't want you to be independent and alone. Yes, you may be in a season of independence, but your heart doesn't have to be. You can use this time to become more dependent on God so that he can prepare you for the man who is out there looking for you.

For those of you who are in a marriage but still don't feel secure enough to be dependent, it's prayer time. It's time to pray that God would change your husband into a man who can be trusted with your precious gift of vulnerability. Keep in mind that your husband may be used to you being strong and independent in marriage, so you may have to make him aware that you want to be more dependent. It's okay to need and ask him for help. Let him know, Sis. You came into this thing super independent, but after a while, your mind and body will help you to realize why you weren't created to be. When we choose well, or allow God to change our husbands, we can feel comfortable being vulnerable and depending on our husbands. Sis, I'm so glad I have no shame in wanting to be dependent. It has taken a lot of work and patience to get here. Trust me, I still have things to reprogram, but I'm trying to relinquish control. So, again, you must evaluate your mindset and misconceptions. Consider how you were raised and how you saw men treated or valued. Did you really have an example of a healthy picture of a godly husband and wife relationship? Did you see women in healthy dating relationships? How can you adjust your mindset, desires, and choices to shift into a healthy form of independence? You can do it. WE can do it.

Disagreement vs Hate

Calling out sin for what it is can come off as offensive to some. Not only is it offensive to non-believers, but some Christians are also offended when called out on sin. In the Bible, pride is defined as elevating one's opinions and thoughts above God's authoritative Word. This is exactly what we're doing when we think our opinions and feelings are the deciding factor for what God considers sin. We position our own views above God when we give certain sins a pass because we find ourselves or a loved one wrapped up in them. For example, I would love to overeat without feeling the consequences, but God's Word considers gluttony a sin. Look around, 69% of Americans are overweight or obese. Do you think God wants us to deal with all the sickness, disease, and limitations that come with that condition? No, he wants us to live healthy lives, but when we talk about gluttony, many Christians would rather minimize it than strive for self-control.

Another way culture influences us is by normalizing sin and shaming believers for being in disagreement. Hate is defined as an intense dislike or disgust for something or someone. To disagree means to have a different opinion. I can remember moments in my life when I expressed regret for having an abortion at the age of 20 to those within the church. I opened up about how that sin had impacted my mind and body at the time, and how deceived I was when I made the decision out of convenience. People felt that by expressing my feelings of regret, I was being judgmental and hateful toward women, even though I had committed the very same sin. I have learned that the principles of sin don't go away just because I participated in those sins. Sin is sin, no matter who commits it. In fact, after I was forgiven, I wanted to encourage more women to make different decisions. The enemy hopes we will remain silent about our convictions and mistakes, but who does that help? When we cover up past sins or remain silent when asked about our beliefs on controversial topics, we miss opportunities to minister God's love and truth to others. You are not a hater simply because you disagree. In fact, it's an expression of love for people when you don't condone or encourage their nonsense. Think about it: Can I truly love you if I encourage you to keep living in sin? If I choose to agree with your feelings and actions that go against what God says, I'm setting you up for failure. I look at it this way: there are many people in life who will agree with everything we do. I'd rather be known as the person you can count on to tell you the truth, even if it doesn't feel good all the time.

It's time to stop trusting culture to lead us. It's time to start being led by the Holy Spirit. Living a life of doing whatever you want, or however the culture influences you, will not result in a life of peace, happiness, or success. We need boundaries. We need principles to live by so we don't have to trust our culture's jacked-up understanding of right and wrong. Think about it right now: Who or what has been guiding your life up to this point? Do you like where your mindset, values, and ungodly desires (we all have them) have gotten you? At this rate, where is your life headed? The most important question is, are your desires in line with the will of God for your life? Whether we know it or not, God has a specific plan and purpose for our lives. The more you get to know Him, the clearer His plan will become. Jeremiah 29:11 says, "For I know the plans I have for you," declares the Lord, "plans to prosper you and not to harm you, plans to give you hope and a future." Regardless of what we've done in the past, that plan is still in God's heart for us. He's waiting for us to let go of our worldly ambitions and desires to focus on His desire for us. At the very foundation of His plan is us being worthy women. As we ask Him to heal our hearts and minds, our outward behavior changes. Following God's principles will add value to our lives that material possessions cannot. No, we don't just wake up one morning doing everything right and pleasing God. Change is a daily commitment to being intentional about how we live when no one is watching. God sees everything we do in private and rewards us publicly in His due time. We must make a commitment to step away from culture and into God's perfect will for our lives. Go ahead and say it with me, Sis... God, I'm serious this time.

Let's Reflect

Who were you most influenced by as a teen (Favorite singer, adult, friend) ? Was their behavior positive or negative?

_____

_____

_____

_____

What cultural influence resonated with you the most? Why is it important that you allow God to influence you in that area instead?

How do you want your mindset to shift? Are you willing to be seen as different for the sake of being more like Christ in your thinking and living?

Lets Pray.

Lord, I need You! Help me recognize the areas in my life that reflect the culture and not You. Help me change my worldly desires so that I can desire the things You want for me. Thank You for Your mercy and grace as I lived life without considering Your principles and plan for me. Change the way I see my worth. Help me learn what it means to be a woman of value in the Kingdom of God. Help me become that woman. I forgive myself for the things I've done that I'm not proud of, and I thank You for forgiving me. Help me see my value in the way that You see it. Thank You for loving me and opening my eyes to the ways I have been deceived by culture and the world I live in. Help me recognize when I'm doing what I want and not what You want. Help me trust and become dependent on You and the plan You have for my life.

In Jesus' Name,

Amen

Chapter 4

Becoming the New You...

This means that anyone who belongs to Christ has become a new person. The old life is gone; a new life has begun!

2 Corinthians 5:17

Ok, so this "New You" that we're about to talk about... She is already inside you. You just haven't tapped into her yet. It's very easy to convince yourself that there is no need for change, or that it's too late to change the trajectory of your life. The idea of becoming a "new you" requires humility. It forces you to be real about the fact that maybe you've been going about life the wrong way. Maybe you got so caught up in living life that you forgot how special you are to God and that He created you for a specific purpose. Or, you may find yourself in a space of having accomplished what you wanted but still feel as though something is missing. In my own life, I was so concerned with trying to survive mentally and emotionally that I couldn't imagine God having a purpose for my life. I couldn't see God's heart toward me, but one day, God placed Pastor Sabrina Nero in my life to help me see past all my struggles and speak to the potential that was lying dormant inside me. I remember being in one of the darkest seasons of my life after the abortion and getting ready to deploy to Iraq. I went up to the altar for prayer, and during that moment, she spoke these words to me:

> *"God is going to use you to speak to women, but you have to carry yourself in a way that God will be able to get the glory."*

Even though I had no idea how it would ever happen, I received what she said in my heart. At that moment, her words made absolutely no sense to me, but I now realize that those words had a purpose. Here I was, depressed, still processing an abortion, and emotionally distraught because my toxic relationship was ending, but somehow, God was going to use **ME** to speak to women. Truth is, He sure was, and He used her words to call me to a higher standard of living.

The thing about the old you is that she becomes very familiar. She seems to have your best interests in mind. A part of you really wants to trust that your old ways of thinking and behaving are going to yield better results. It often feels like you are stuck in this place of feeling comfortable with the old you, but you are also fearful of where doing things differently will lead you. The idea of becoming this "new you" sounds really good, but you wrestle with the question, where do I even start? How do you actually walk this thing out on a daily basis? How do you begin to grow spiritually so that God can begin to change your life? There is no step-by-step guide… or is there? When I look back at my call to action to "live in a way that will allow God to get the Glory", I had no idea at the time what that meant. As a new "serious" Christian woman, I was ready to bring Him glory, but I often ended up doing the opposite. I had found this amazing church that was ready to teach me all I needed to know about living Holy, but then I was thrown into the desert of Iraq to figure it out on my own. The step-by-step guide, also known as the Bible, was in my possession the entire year, but I didn't spend much time reading it. I thought that, surely, if God wanted me to know how to be a better woman, He was going to send someone to teach, mentor, and coach me on how to do it. I really thought that change was just going to happen. I spent an entire year with God on my mind, but I made no real effort to allow Him INTO my heart and mind. I don't want that for you. You're excited about changing, and the best way to start seeing that change is getting serious about connecting with God for yourself. Yes, building a relationship with Him that is not dependent on someone else spoon-feeding you ways to change. You're reading this book right now, but don't forget that if these tips should fail you, God's word never fails! So, let's talk about what has to happen for you to start seeing God move in your life.

You Must Pray

It's crazy! When I look back on my life prior to knowing God, the one thing I always knew how to do was pray and beg God for the things I wanted. I would say, *"Dear Lord, It's me again."* God to death! I was one of those people who only came to God when I needed something. Even today, if I'm not careful, prayer is the first spiritual discipline that will slip my mind. You know how it goes. You lay down, excited to pray, only to wake up and realize you never finished the prayer. Trust me, it's a very powerful tool, but complacency and tiredness often make it easy to set prayer on the back burner of life. However, we must remember that prayer gives us direct access to God. Imagine being able to pick up your phone, call the only true and living God, and have an entire conversation with Him. We would be so confident that whatever we discussed would be taken care of because we actually talked to God. Well, prayer is just like a phone conversation.

When we take the time to talk to God, He is listening. The most important thing when engaged in prayer is that you keep it real with God. We have a tendency to keep our worst thoughts, feelings, fears, and temptations hidden from people and God. We fear that if they knew the things that really cross our minds, they would view us differently. Yes, that may be the case with people, so I do urge intentionality about who we share our hearts with. However, unlike humans, we don't have to worry about hiding our true selves from God. He already knows all about our worst things, but He wants us to trust Him to help us work them out. Do you really think you can get rid of lust yourself? Do you really think you can ignore the fact that deep down you genuinely hate your father, or are jealous of someone because they seem to be doing better than you? No Ma'am. When we allow those things to stay tucked away in our hearts, they put down roots. Prayer is our way of telling God that we acknowledge that those hard things exist, and we need Him to help us clear them out. As we start to share the hidden things of our hearts, we will feel a sense of freedom, knowing that He loves us, even in the areas where we don't love ourselves.

Our prayers to God don't have to be super elaborate or drawn out. God just wants us to trust Him with the things He already knows. Some people get intimidated because they've heard other people go super deep, and there's a time for that, but we just need to get comfortable sharing our hearts with God. Matthew 6:5-8 reassures us that God doesn't need us to make a show of prayer. It should be intimate and transparent, as though you're talking to a trusted close friend. I love how The Message version explains this text:

> *"And when you come before God, don't turn that into a theatrical production either. All these people making a regular show out of their prayers, hoping for fifteen minutes of fame! Do you think God sits in a box seat?*
>
> *6 "Here's what I want you to do: Find a quiet, secluded place so you won't be tempted to role-play before God. Just be there as simply and honestly as you can manage. The focus will shift from you to God, and you will begin to sense his grace.*
>
> *7-13 "The world is full of so-called prayer warriors who are prayer-ignorant. They're full of formulas and programs and advice, peddling techniques for getting what you want from God. Don't fall for that nonsense. This is your Father you are dealing with,*

and he knows better than you what you need. With a God like this loving you, you can pray very simply.
Matthew 6:5-8 (MSG)

So, keep it simple, Sis, but let's commit to making our prayer time with God consistent and honest. We should seek Him not only when we need something but simply because God wants us to cast the things we care about on Him (1 Peter 5:7). You are not a burden to Him. You are not wasting His time. This Father is excited to hear from you, and even more excited to speak back to you. The more time you spend in prayer, the more clearly you'll be able to recognize when God is speaking to or nudging you. He'll bring scriptures or principles to your mind that will help you make better decisions and bring comfort to you in situations that may not be moving how you'd like.

Prayer Prompts

You don't have to be on your knees to pray, Sis. Turn off the radio and talk to your daddy while you drive. Keep it real with Him, tell Him your plans, and pray for the people that you love. Pray for your children and their future. Pray that God would draw them into a closer relationship with Him. Pray for your spouse and the hidden things they may be dealing with. Ask God to give you wisdom on how to deal with people you find it hard to like. Pray for your family members who can still be saved. Ask God to draw them closer and believe that it's not too late for them. Pray before you go into your job. Ask God for wisdom to help you excel in your work and overcome any obstacles you may be facing. Girl, you can even pray for your boss and co-workers. Ask God to move in the lives of those who seem to be struggling.

Here are some prompts to help you start your prayers....

- Is there a person you want God to deliver?
- Pray for your siblings and extended family to come to know God.
- Pray for deliverance from addictions that have plagued your family.
- Pray that God would remove all generational curses in the name of Jesus.
- Pray that God would bless you with wisdom and spiritual discernment.
- Is there a situation that you feel God has forgotten?
- Is there someone you need to forgive?

- Is there someone that you've hurt that may not have forgiven you?

- Pray for your kids' future careers, purpose, and spouses.

- Pray for your husband's faith to be strengthened and his confidence to lead your home.

- Pray that God will increase your respect for your husband.

- Pray for your future husband, and that God is preparing him for you.

- Pray that God would heal you from past hurt so you can be open to love again.

- Pray that God will comfort your children that do not have their father present at home.

- Pray for your children's self-esteem and their desire to have a relationship with God.

Read Your Word

How can we know what God expects of us if we never read His Word? Girl, I remember there were nights when I would open the Bible and instantly get sleepy. I experienced some of that sleepiness because of the time I was choosing to read, and some of it was because I felt like what I was reading was hard to understand. I was going to church and listening to sermons, so in my mind, it was acceptable if I didn't consistently read the Word for myself. I was so wrong. Yes, it was good that I was consuming reliable content, but God also wanted to speak directly to me through the pages of His Word. I've listened to many sermons that have blown my spiritual mind, but reading a word that God leads me to in my private time just feels personal. I also realized that I didn't have a strategy. I would open the Bible and just read wherever I landed. While I've experienced a few mind-blowing moments using this method, things were never consistent.

Now, I go about reading the Bible a couple of different ways. I find a study plan based on what I am dealing with and work through it on the YouVersion Bible app. This guides me toward passages that can speak to my immediate spiritual need. Plans are a good way for you to stay consistent and intentional about dealing with the issues and struggles you are facing. I also like to study what God expects of me. Yes, he wants me to work through my struggles, but sometimes we are struggling because we are walking in disobedience. The fruit of the Spirit is a great place to start learning what God expects of us as believers. After you finish studying love, joy, peace, patience, kindness, goodness, faithfulness, gentleness, and self-control (Galatians 5:22-23), you'll be seeing life through a new lens. I encourage you to do a thorough study on each individual word and see how it directs you to adjust your mind, attitude, and life. Girl, you'll start to see just how much work there is to be done on this journey and grow more excited to do it. Learning what God expects of us through His Word has the capability to show us how we fall short so that we can make adjustments. God also will reveal to us the opposite of these things and what He doesn't want us to do. He'll show us how the works of the flesh are the things that get us all jacked up. For example, God will reveal things such as sexual immorality, impurity, sensuality, idolatry, sorcery, enmity, strife, jealousy, fits of anger, rivalries, dissensions, divisions, 21envy, drunkenness, orgies, and things like these (Galatians 5:19-21).

When studying God's word, I usually take it one word at a time. For example, this is how I would begin a study on the works of the flesh. I would take the first word, *jealousy,* and look up the definition. Then I would continue to define words in the definition that have a deeper meaning. After that, I'd google scriptures about jealousy and write down the ones that speak to me. Then, I'd journal about areas I'm struggling with within that area. This would allow me to tell God and identify within myself specific areas in which sin is operating. After confession, I'd then look up scriptures to help me overcome the sin. I've found that reading blogs, books, and sermons after I study helps me to gain more knowledge and retain information about the specific sin. You can simply search *"scriptures to overcome jealousy"* and look on YouTube for *"sermons* about jealousy". Sis, I've given you an example below of what study usually looks like for me:

- Jealousy - feeling or showing envy of someone or their achievements and advantages
- Envy- a feeling of discontented or resentful longing aroused by someone else's possessions, qualities, or luck.
- Discontented- dissatisfied, especially with one's circumstances.

James 4:2-3 (ESV) - You desire and do not have, so you murder. You covet and cannot obtain, so you fight and quarrel. You do not have, because you do not ask. You ask and do not receive, because you ask wrongly, to spend it on your passions.

James 3: 14-15 (ESV)- But if you have bitter jealousy and selfish ambition in your hearts, do not boast and be false to the truth. This is not the wisdom that comes down from above, but is earthly, unspiritual, demonic.

Romans 13:13 (NASB)- Let us behave properly as in the day, not in carousing and drunkenness, not in sexual promiscuity and sensuality, not in strife and jealousy.

How has jealousy shown up in my life? Sometimes, I find myself envious of marriages that seem spiritually healthy. I get frustrated that my husband isn't as serious about God as some other women's spouses are. Even though he is a good husband in all other aspects, this one hangs me up at times. This leads me to feeling discontent and frustrated that God isn't working fast enough. Like, I want him to be serious about God today and forget that God is waiting on him, just like He waited on me. I sometimes get jealous that my business or ambitions haven't taken off as fast as other people I follow. I feel like my product is just as good, so it leads me to questioning God's timing (again). These feelings of jealousy have me focusing on myself and not trusting God and His timing.

How do I overcome jealousy? Remember **Jeremiah 29:11** (NIV)- "For I know the plans I have for you," declares the Lord, "plans to prosper you and not to harm you, plans to give you hope and a future." I have to trust that God's plan for me is better than the idea and timeline that I have set for myself. I must remember that He has the same great plans for the person I'm jealous or envious of. Lord, help me recognize when I'm feeling jealous or envious. If someone is making me feel envious or jealous, I need to recognize it, step away (stop watching their content), and ask You to help me be happy for them and trust your plan for me. Take away the fear of not reaching my goals when I see others reaching theirs faster. Help me to trust your timing and remember that my goals are just a suggestion for you. I know that you know when and what is best, so help me to remember that in moments of jealousy. Thank you for helping me see the things that are hindering me from truly being happy for others and trusting you completely with my life.

After completing my study, I listen to sermons on the same topic so that God can show me different perspectives. I know it seems like a lot to learn, but remember, God's word is intended to help show us the hidden and obvious places in our hearts, minds, and behavior that need work. The only way to do that is by studying. As you grow to maturity in your time of study, there will be times when reading an entire book of the Bible is necessary. It allows us to gain context that a single scripture doesn't provide. It allows us to see the humanity of people and gain more insight into their experiences. For example, when you read the book of Job, you learn how he had everything but was allowed by God to be tested by the devil. God had so much confidence in Job's faith that He knew no circumstance could make him turn on God. Satan literally took everything from him, tortured his body with sickness, and allowed his friends to turn on him. We see him on an emotional roller coaster, telling God how he feels, questioning why he was born, reminding himself of his innocence, only to start wallowing in the raw feelings of neglect by God. Job's wife couldn't even understand why he continued to maintain his integrity. Out of frustration with his circumstances, his wife said to him:

> *"Are you still maintaining your integrity? Curse God and die!" [10] He replied, "You are talking like a foolish[b] woman. Shall we accept good from God, and not trouble?"* **Job 2:9-10 (NIV).**

This look into Job's life shows the reality of how bad things can get for us, yet we are still expected to trust God. We see that Job was angry, depressed, discouraged, and at times a complainer, but he did not give up on God. I'm not sure about you, but I've been through seasons that don't even come close to what Job experienced and didn't handle as well as Job did. God allowed this story in the Bible so that we could see just how bad things got for Job and observe how he maintained his faith in God. Without context, it is easy to believe that God was being unfair to Job; however, God ended up blessing Job tremendously at the end of his suffering. My point here is that reading an entire book of the Bible has benefits that are not found in a single scripture or topical study. Now, I know this is a lot to take in, especially if you are new to your Bible reading journey. However, I just want to encourage you to start. While the Bible is amazing, jumping right into all of its chapters may not be the best idea if the goal is to stay interested and avoid getting overwhelmed. So, pray and ask God how and where you should start getting into His Word. When you feel drawn to a certain topic or book of the Bible, start there. The first few scriptures may not immediately captivate you, but give it time. Go at your own pace, and ask God to help you understand what you are reading and how to apply what you've read to your life.

While writing this book, God revealed to me how important it is to begin memorizing scripture as well. I often say, *"I haven't memorized the verse, but the* Bible *talks about..."*. While my intentions are good, there's still a level of uncertainty present when not knowing the scripture references. I often feel more confident when I can refer to a scripture and not just take my or someone else's word for it. I once thought that recalling the scriptures wasn't that serious, but I now know that it's easy to slip into doubt when we don't have the facts concerning the Word readily available in our memory. Think about it. When Satan spoke to Eve, he was able to manipulate her understanding of the scripture because she was not completely sure about what God said.

"You will not surely die," the serpent told her" ***(Genesis 3:4).***

Now, she had just told him what God said, but because she wasn't completely sure that God's word was true, she allowed Satan to deceive her. Many of us have been in the same situation, if we are honest. We have found ourselves being deceived by the enemy because we don't fully remember what God's Word says. We can't afford to be in those situations anymore. I feel so confident when I speak the word of God that I have memorized and held in my heart and mind. Nothing beats the godly confidence that comes from knowing His Word is true, and not a devil in hell or on earth being able to convince you otherwise. Knowing the Word of God eliminates fear and doubt. There will be times when we'll need scripture but won't have access to a Bible. Memorizing the scriptures allows us to be prepared at all times. Trust me, Sis, knowing the Word of God can change your life. How do I know? It's changing mine.

Set Some Boundaries

You already know the things that will cause you to revert back to your old ways. Below, I'm going to have you identify some of the things that need to change for you. If we don't set boundaries, we will end up right back in the same places where God is freeing us from. We will find ourselves saying our favorite line, "God, I'm serious this time," all while knowing we don't really mean it. It's time to take accountability for the things we have the ability to control. You can keep lying to yourself about wanting to be different, but pretty soon, you will stop believing in yourself.

There's a whole term for not becoming the person we really want to be: cognitive dissonance. It is the space between who we are and who we want to be. When there is too much space between the two (dissonance), we start to freak out mentally and feel like frauds. At that point, we either lower the bar, do what needs to be done to close the gap, or get rid of the goal entirely. Girl, this definition exposed me to myself in so many ways. It's so much easier to lower the bar or throw the entire bar away when we struggle to become who God calls us to be. Instead of setting up boundaries that help us reach our goals, we get rid of the goal. Think about it. What is one thing that you want for yourself, but you keep lowering or removing the bar? Is it to be a more patient, present mom? Are you supposed to be saving yourself for the man God is preparing for you? Is it becoming financially stable? We all have a few areas that could use some more clear boundaries. I really need you to understand that these boundaries are to help you live your best life. In fact, boundaries are the key to ensuring that you live your best life. When establishing boundaries, the first thing you need to do is be honest about the things and areas that you want to change. Ensure that this is not done jokingly or with a spirit of disbelief. Sometimes, we don't even have the courage to set a goal for fear of failing again. Joking about it makes your boundary-setting time feel less serious, while deep down, you know that changing this one thing would make you feel a thousand times better.

Let's be real. You don't think you can really set boundaries, so you downplay the process. Well, not anymore, Sis. I want to challenge you here. Think of one thing that you want to do and be very clear about what it is. Yes, stop reading right now and think of your one thing. It can be to register for a class, lose 10 pounds, pay off a credit card, or pray every morning. We all have at least one thing we've been struggling to accomplish; the choice is yours.

My goal is to:

_____
_____
_____
_____
_____
_____
_____

Now that you've clearly identified one goal, it's time to identify your why...

I need to do this because:

_____

_____

_____

_____

I've quit in the past because:

_____

_____

_____

_____

If I'm going to accomplish this, I need to : (insert a boundary that you need to set and stick and BE VERY CLEAR.

_____

_____

Sis, if you are going to make progress toward the things you want to accomplish, you have to set some boundaries. You need boundaries in your relationships, finances, diet, career, and personal goals. If you have been a quitter in the past, you have to be honest about your tendencies and look out for old ways of thinking that make you feel comfortable about quitting. We also have to consider our strengths and weaknesses. Because organization is my weakness, I have to make lists and reminders to stay on task. I literally have to tell myself no in order to avoid taking on additional projects that stretch me so thin that I don't complete the things on my list. So, if like me, spreading yourself too thin is an issue for you, you have to learn to prioritize your commitments. As much as I want to work on my jewelry business, I've had to decide that it's not a priority right now. I will get back to that once I complete the commitments I've already made for this year. What about you? Are you obligated to do so many things that you haven't seen progress in the most important areas? Keep in mind that there will be seasons of life that require us to be stretched thin, like getting adjusted to having a baby or starting a new job. But, always feeling overwhelmed is not healthy or necessary and signals a need for a boundary. Say it with me: "I CAN'T DO IT ALL!"

    I know you think you can, but be honest with yourself. Have you exceeded your capacity, or are you unorganized? Putting things on the back burner doesn't mean you have failed; it just means that you have learned to prioritize. For example, I took a couple of years off from school because I knew that adding school to my plate would overwhelm me mentally and physically. Once I put the effort into managing my current priorities, I eventually felt comfortable adding one college course to my plate. I still experienced a bit of overwhelm, but as I intentionally made homework a part of my weekly routine, things felt better. I planned take-out dinners for days that assignments were due so that I could have more time to feed my family without feeling rushed when getting my assignments submitted. When I initially decided to take a break from school, I felt a sense of failure, but the weight that was lifted off my shoulders was so refreshing. Yes, that meant I would be a little later getting my degree, but the timeline I initially gave myself didn't take into consideration my lack of capacity to add the additional workload to my already full plate. So, I chose to trust God and let those feelings of failure fade.

So, I'm encouraging you to assess your life. Set some boundaries for yourself. If you know you take on too much, only allow yourself to have two additional tasks to work on at a time. This is a boundary. My personality naturally seeks approval and validation through accomplishments. That can drive me to take on way too much, and then I get down when I don't accomplish all the things I set out to accomplish. Each month I give myself goals (boundaries) to work on, and at the end of the month, I review them. You may need to do this weekly or monthly according to the boundaries you are setting. Boundaries are intended to hold you back in a healthy way because sometimes, without restraints, we get out of alignment with the goals and intentions we've set. Boundaries also require discipline. Discipline is the ability to do something even when you don't "want" or "feel" like doing it. Keep discipline in mind when you are tempted to move or disregard your boundary. Remember, your boundaries are for yourself and others. When people know where you stand, they can make a conscious decision to respect your boundaries. Set some boundaries, Sis. We all need them if we are going to change.

Create Routines that Keep You on Track

Ok, this next principle is a game changer, or at least it has been for me. Setting routines has helped me to save time when thinking about what needs to be done in my life. In the Army, we call it a "battle rhythm". It's defined as a deliberate daily cycle of activities intended to synchronize current and future operations. I believe we could all benefit from synchronizing current and future things we have going on in our lives. Now, I have not perfected this yet, but hear me when I say, routines have increased my productivity and taken away some of the chaos in our home. My son knows that before he goes to sleep, the kitchen must be cleaned, and all dishes must be washed. I give him the freedom to choose the time, as long as it is complete when I wake up. My husband and I have worked out a nighttime routine for Taj (kinda lol). He takes care of giving him a bath and preparing him for bed. After months of trying to get consistent with my skincare routine, I have finally done it. I made skincare a part of my shower routine each night to eliminate me having to think about it separately. This concept is known as habit stacking. Habit stacking is defined as combining a new habit with something you already do consistently. Sometimes I don't "feel" like keeping up my routines, but I stopped making it optional. I hop out of the shower and head straight to the sink to do my skin and tie up my hair. Girl, I even put on a nightly lip butter without even thinking about it. It really feels good to know that I'm prioritizing myself in these simple ways. I go to bed feeling so good about myself, and it's all due to this simple change in habits.

I've also noticed that my mornings are so much better when I prepare the night before. I know you've probably heard this a thousand times, but let this be another sign that you need to try it. I find all the outfits, pack all the bags, and even pre-pack my lunch for the next day, so that all I have to do is grab and go. My mornings have become seamless since I started to take care of all these things at night. Before developing a morning routine, most of the time I woke up feeling rushed and confused about what to wear or what I was going to eat for lunch. By the time I made it out of the house, the house looked like a tornado had hit it. Then, I'd have to come home to a messy house where all of my obligations felt like a burden. Basically, I wouldn't want to do anything because there was too much to do. Girl, what I'm trying to tell you is that yes, it may take a few extra minutes to prepare before bed, but that preparation sets you up for a peaceful morning.

Think about your mornings as they are right now. Are you all over the place, frustrated, and late? Or, are you prepared, peaceful, and ready to attack the day? If you think your mornings could use more peace and ease, try working on your nighttime routine. You can be nicer to the kids when you are not frustrated and rushing. When our mornings start off rough due to a lack of preparation, we start our days feeling incompetent. So, take a moment to reflect on your average day. Have you been sabotaging yourself every day by failing to prepare? Keep in mind there are levels to this.

My sixty-year-old retired military coworker has a morning routine that seems nearly impossible to attain. I have to remember that I am called to do the best that I can for my life and not be tempted to mimic his routine. He motivates me, though, because I get to see the results of his discipline firsthand. Seeing how he operates in routines has definitely inspired me to step up my game. So, here is the call for you to step yours up too. Think about the areas of your life that could benefit from a routine, and start making small changes that you can do repeatedly and easily. I'm telling you, Sis, this is the key to getting a little more peace in your life. Synchronizing our lives shows us where we have space to add in new things.

This year, God asked me to give up social media, and that sacrifice has shown me just how much time I was giving to social media. I was wasting time looking at other people accomplishing their goals and telling myself I didn't have time to accomplish mine. Since then, I've been setting monthly goals and revisiting them each month. Monitoring my goals and routines is showing me where I'm not taking action and where to hold myself accountable throughout the month in order to improve. You can use this same strategy to make your day a little more peaceful. When I start my day peacefully, it opens my mind and heart to make worship a part of my morning. It is a challenge to worship when I haven't prepared and my day starts off rough and rushed. I know that some level of anger and frustration is sometimes unavoidable, but if we're being honest, there are times we can totally avoid it by being more intentional about how we use our time. I'm telling you, Sis, you have to make time for God and yourself by decluttering your life, establishing routines, and setting boundaries. Ok, I know I just got real deep talking about routines, but it's real. I want to enjoy a life that doesn't feel rushed. This thing is a struggle at times, but I'm determined to push through. Keep trying! Nevertheless, I can do it! You can do it, Sis!

Bring it all Together.

Now, before you leave this chapter feeling motivated to change your life, implement your routines, and level up your prayer life, just know there will be resistance. There will be spiritual and physical resistance that is determined to discourage you to the point of quitting this journey of becoming the best version of yourself. Your kids and spouse may not be on board with all the new routines, but change is tough for everyone, so **Don't**

Quit! You will get it wrong often, and at times feel inauthentic for trying new things and stretching your norms. The more you embrace these changes and behaviors, the more natural they will become. Push through the feelings of self-doubt. Now that you're attempting to level up and be led by God, the enemy doesn't like that. You will be tempted more than ever to revert back to your old ways, but keep in mind that's a part of Satan's strategy. 1 Peter 5:8 (KJV) says, *"Be sober, be vigilant, because your adversary the devil walketh about as a roaring lion, seeking whom he may devour."*

    I hate to break it to you, Sis, but he wants to devour you, but you serve a God that even Satan himself must answer to. Knowing this should encourage you to not be deceived when it looks like Satan is winning. When he tries to make you feel like trash for slipping up, remind him and yourself that God's mercy is everlasting. All you have to do is repent to God and make a genuine effort to get it right next time. Listen, there is no hope for satan so his goal is to make you think there is no hope for you. That's a lie. Romans 5:8 says, *"But God demonstrates his own love for us in this: While we were still sinners, Christ died for us."* That's you and me, Sis. God's love for us is the real reason he's a hater. So, just be prepared for the schemes of Satan, and know that his attacks are only going to make you stronger in your faith.

I'm not trying to scare you, but you need to know that as you start trying to change, the enemy will be coming for you! He has even tried to come for me while writing this book because he knows that you and thousands of other women are bound to get set free. I've had to encourage myself and keep it moving. So, be encouraged and keep going, Sis.

Now What?... It's time to Work!

Now, it's time to put these things into action. It's time to get clear about who you want to become, and developing a personal vision statement may help. A personal vision statement describes the person you want to become in the future by stating your strengths, values, and goals. This statement is not really about who you are now, but a picture of how you want to show up in the world in the future. You may not have all the answers right now, but you should have a baseline for the things you would like to see yourself embody going forward as this "New" You. So, let's practice. I want you to take a moment to envision the best version of yourself. Yes, like close your eyes and see yourself living life in a way that feels good and pleases God. How do you feel mentally? Where do you work? Who's around you? What is your work schedule like? What kind of car do you drive? What does your home look and feel like? How do you look physically? What is most of your time spent doing? Don't rush this process. Take a day or so to think about how you want to change. Reflect on the things you know need to change, and include the changed and improved version of yourself in your personal vision statement. Before you move on to the next chapter, complete this exercise below.

What are your strengths?

(example: compassionate, loyal, disciplined, motivated, good writer, signing, helping people, creative, style, fitness, motivated, self-starter, organized)

_____

_____

_____

_____

_____

What are your values? (honesty, health, faith, respect, kindness, dependability, perseverance, growth, wealth, health).

_____

_____

_____

What are you most happy doing?

_____

_____

_____

_____

What do you want to be remembered for?

_____

_____

_____

_____

Here is my personal vision statement...

> *I want to be a woman of character. I want to keep gaining educational and spiritual knowledge that will*

allow me to pour into others. I want my husband and sons to call me blessed, and know they can trust that I will always support and encourage them. I want to inspire those around me to desire a life of faith and mental and physical wellness. Ultimately, I want God to be pleased with my life as I walk in the purpose that He created me for.

Whew! You did it! You have created your personal vision statement. Keep in mind that this will adjust as your mindset and goals shift. You should put this somewhere that you can easily find it when you need a reminder of the woman you want to become. I believe that even if you don't know who she is just yet, getting a closer relationship with the Creator will help you determine exactly why He created you. You have a purpose, and I believe that starts with simply surrendering to become a good woman according to God's standard. Reading your word, setting boundaries, praying, and embracing healing will all lead you to discover your God-given purpose. You just have to be willing to do the work.

Let's Pray.

Lord, thank you for being a consistent and loving God. Thank you for loving me at my worst and still maintaining your vision for me at my best. Thank you for helping me realize my need for more of you and for giving me a desire to be a better woman. I pray that you would forgive me for the things I've done and the old mindset that has tried to make me think that I know better than you. Help me to seek you diligently and give me a desire to learn your Word and make it a part of who I am. Now, Lord, as I strive to become a better woman, I need you more than ever. Help me to see myself the way you see me. You said in Psalms 139:14 that I am fearfully and wonderfully made. Help me to believe that when I don't feel that way. Place women in my life who will be godly examples for me. Show me the areas that I need healing and help me to take action to start the healing process. Thank you for being patient with me, Lord. Help me to be patient with myself. I thank you for the woman that I am becoming.

In Jesus' Name

Amen

Chapter 5

Sneaky Things That Hinder Your Growth

Submit yourselves therefore to God. Resist the devil, and he will flee from you. **James 4:7**

Y.O.U. (Your Own Understanding)

Girl, I couldn't send you on your way without mentioning some of the things that distract us from seeing our vision statements come to life. Off top, the sneakiest distraction of them all is YOU. Following **Your Own Understanding** will lead you to live a life that's based on your feelings, emotions, and human rationale instead of being led by God. The bible tells us in Proverbs 3:5-6 (NIV) *"Trust in the Lord with all your heart and lean not on your own understanding; in all your ways submit to him, and he will make your paths straight"*.

Contrary to this scripture, there was a time when the first thing I would do was lean on my own understanding. I'd make decisions and consider my bad behavior acceptable based on the standards I'd developed in the past. I wasn't running stuff by God prior to doing it. Let me tell you, the more you allow God to change you, the more you'll realize that your way of thinking is usually tainted by past experiences, ungodly thought processes, and the pull of your flesh. You are the deciding factor in how you execute your vision! So, before you go telling the devil he can't stop you, you need to make sure YOU don't stop yourself. You have been living your life the same way for years, so it's comfortable at this point. Even if you don't like the outlook of your current ways of thinking, it's still safe and familiar.

Note that this journey you're headed on will not always be comfortable and can also be unpredictable, if I'm honest. There will be a lot of forcing yourself to think, act, and feel differently, but this is how you gain control of your flesh. The easiest way to hinder your spiritual growth in God is by attempting to transform in your own power and become a better person without allowing the Holy Spirit to lead and guide you. We often forget about how God tells us to SUBMIT to HIM, so that we can resist the devil. It's hard to resist the devil when we are not submitted to God because we are tempted by Satan many times throughout our day. So the question becomes, what does it really look like to submit to God?

Good Question! Here are some basic principles we can use to begin really submitting to God. As you begin to read, your immediate thought may be, "Girl, please," but that's the old you trying to protect you from the unknown, even when it means going against God's word.

Basic Principles that Help Us Submit to God

- Give up your desires and feelings that do not align with God.
  (Galatians 5:24)
- Be mindful about where you go and what you do with your body.
  (1 Corinthians 3:16)
- Distance yourself from bad friends and family. (1 Corinthians 15:33-34 Amplified)
- Think about your thoughts, and be careful not to fill your mind with anti-God rhetoric. (Philippians 4:8)
- Be kind and friendly. (Proverbs 18:24)

- Accept and attempt to live differently than life without Christ. (Ephesians 4:22-32)
- Forgive people that have harmed you and let you down. (Ephesians 4:32)
- Reprogram your mind to obey God and not the things your body tells you (Romans 8:7-8)

Regardless of how long we've been saved, it's important to be reminded of these principles. Just because I'm getting it right today doesn't mean I'll have it right tomorrow. Obedience to God is a daily effort. The journey toward obedience is filled with getting it wrong, asking God for forgiveness, and trying again. If we start to feel like we've got it all together, that's usually a sign that we need to examine our hearts and behaviors. How are we treating those closest to us? How are our attitudes? Are we holding on to something that makes us hostile toward someone? Are there any habits that are slowly turning into addictions without us realizing it? Answering these questions from time to time allows us to check in with ourselves to see how we're bringing the sneaky areas of our flesh into submission.

Social Media

The next sneaky distraction is social media. I've seen this hinder children, middle-aged adults, and older adults as well. Social media can be a breeding ground for comparison, jealousy, demonic influences, and the wasting of time if we are not careful. It's crazy how time seems to fly when we get on those apps. I sometimes wake up pumped to be productive, but slowly change my plans after getting caught up in the cycle of social media throughout the day. We've all been there, but the key is recognizing the patterns. How do you feel once you get off? Are you spending more time connecting with your virtual friends than your actual family? That was me. I was so determined to grow all my social media handles and make a "positive impact for the kingdom" that I was neglecting my own family. Our engagement with social media is sneaky because it seems so innocent, and we often don't realize what it's distracting us from. I'm not saying that you have to give it up completely, but I'm asking you to consider if scrolling prevents you from doing things that you say are a priority. Does it interfere with your desire to spend time with God? I could find various excuses to avoid studying the Bible in the morning, but picking up my phone and scrolling through the apps became a natural reflex. I got excited to see who has liked my posts and said great things about me. The validation gained from social media really has a way of making us feel good about ourselves, and that's what keeps us coming back.

Social media can also be an escape from reality. Some people enjoy getting lost in the scroll because it distracts them from being present in a reality that they are unhappy about. This escape feels good in the moment, but once you put the phone down, reality is still there waiting. There were times when I went to social media looking for an escape, but instead left feeling much worse about my own life. I couldn't be happy for people, and thought everyone was lying and unhappy because I was unhappy. I didn't want to share anything about my life because it was a complete mess, but I was willing to get lost in the lives of others. Back in 2015 when I started to feel that way, I decided to take some time away from social media to work on myself without comparing my life to others. It was hard and felt lonely, but it gave me the space to face my reality head-on without trying to portray something different to the masses.

Taking a break from social media also exposed how immature and vulnerable I had become with my emotions. There were times when I felt the urge to tell Facebook everything happening in my life, knowing that it would only provide temporary relief and place everyone in my business. I also knew there were men waiting to see a crack in my relationship, and I'm not sure if my emotions would have allowed me to deny that temptation at the time. I'm just being honest with you, Sis. My faith was shaky, and I was in a rough place mentally and emotionally. Just in case you didn't know, the enemy loves to ruin marriages that way on social media. I've seen it! There is a concept in popular culture called "sliding in the DMs" (Direct Messages), which happens when a person you find attractive sends you a message, and you entertain it. Yeah, it's a whole thing, and people don't care if you're married or not. Of course, it's a choice to say no and ignore advances, but I also know that when you are in a vulnerable emotional state, the enemy will send temptation that looks like a perfect, harmless solution. So, Sis, if you are not in a place to stand firm, get off of social media until you are. The enemy is waiting to catch you in a weak and vulnerable state. You've been warned.

Horoscopes and Witchcraft

Yes, girl, now I'm coming for your horoscopes, tarot cards, sage, crystals, and zodiac signs. I know firsthand of their power to distract. I literally have Sagittarius tattooed on my stomach because I was clueless about how spiritual these signs were. I consider these things sneaky distractions because if we are not careful, we will rely more on our horoscopes than on the leading of the Holy Spirit. I remember the times I'd wake up and check my horoscope for the day instead of praying for guidance from God. I've met people who use their zodiac sign as a crutch for certain character traits, as though God does not have the power to change them. Think about it; these things are powerful if we have faith in them. Some people are deceived into thinking there is no way to change because of how similar their personalities are to their zodiac sign. I believe this is why God is so clear in describing the character we should have as believers. He expects us to exemplify joy, peace, love, patience, kindness, goodness, faithfulness, and self-control. He tells us that others will know we are His followers by the fruit we bear. So, ask yourself, are you bearing the fruit of your zodiac sign or of Christ?

These demonic influences try to subtly convince you of who you are by shaping you into a mold of the horoscope you have come into agreement with. Think about it; the more you read and trust the Bible, the more it changes and molds you. Think of astrology as Satan's counterfeit way of doing the same. The Bible even mentions their accuracy in comparison to the men of God. *When all the magicians, enchanters, astrologers, and fortune-tellers came in, I told them the dream, but they could not tell me what it meant (Daniel 4:7).* These "wise men" used astrology and magic to guide the king, but Daniel gained his wisdom from God. Their wisdom was limited. While they got some things right, there is some insight God reserves for Himself and His children. He reveals things to us as He sees fit and requires us to trust Him when we don't fully understand things. Using horoscopes and zodiac signs gives you a sense of self-discovery and insight that feels empowering, but their power is very limiting. When we trust in these things, we limit the impact that God can have on our character and behavior. The insight gained through these measures is temporary. Isaiah 47: 13-14 says, *"All the advice you receive has made you tired. Where are all your astrologers, those stargazers who make predictions each month? Let them stand up and save you from what the future holds"*. Simply put, the advice you get from these things will always leave you tired and searching for more.

God, as our creator, can help us know and fulfill our purpose, but only when we submit to Him. This can be very challenging; sometimes, it's easy to feel that God doesn't necessarily show up exactly when we want Him to. This leads a lot of people to get into witchcraft because it seems to provide a sense of instant gratification and control. Instead of relying on scripture like *"vengeance is mine, says the Lord"* (Romans 12:19-21), a witch would rather take matters into her own hands and cast a spell.

So, Sis, if you've been dabbling in astrology, it's time to let it go. No more referencing a zodiac sign when talking about yourself to others. Instead, it's time to ask God for forgiveness and thank Him for opening your eyes to such a deceptive distraction. Ask Him to change those traits that you no longer want to be a part of who you are. Ask Him to reveal your true personality and allow you to walk in it boldly. Oh, and pray for the anointing to give others the same grace. There are some people we've automatically disqualified because we've associated them with one of the more "toxic" zodiac signs. Friendly reminder: they're all toxic, and everyone can change. The reality is some people just don't know. I would have never gotten the zodiac engraved on my body if I truly knew the depths of it. So, let's move in grace when dealing with people who are still being influenced by the pull of it. You may be the person to enlighten them and help them receive deliverance from it.

There are many definitions of witchcraft, but the easiest way to define it biblically is rebellion. *"Rebellion is as sinful as witchcraft, and stubbornness as bad as worshiping idols" (1 Samuel 15:23).* Webster defines witchcraft as an act of violent or open resistance to an established government or ruler. So, when we openly resist God (our ruler), we are walking in witchcraft. When we know God has instructed us to do something, and we flat out do what we want, He considers that witchcraft. Another common form of witchcraft is burning sage for spiritual purposes. Maybe you just like the smell of sage and want to burn it in your home—harmless. But if you are using sage to cleanse your environment of evil spirits and negative energy, or to generate wisdom and clarity, it's not as harmless as you think. As we take this walk seriously with God, we have to accept that there won't always be a quick fix to our issues. Yes, it's nice and convenient to think that burning sage could get rid of the evil spirits in your environment. But if God is not in the sage that you believe has so much power, then what spirit is actually cleansing your environment?

If you really want to cleanse your environment, start by removing everything attached to the enemy. Stop allowing your home to be the landing pad where everyone comes to smoke, drink, and have a good time. Examine the type of people you have surrounded yourself with and stop giving them so much access to you. Consider the music you consume, the books you read, and the amount of alcohol you drink. After all, liquor stores refer to their products as "spirits" for a reason. Think about it. Are any of these things subconsciously influencing you? You can determine this by taking note of how you feel after consumption. Does your mood change? Do you regret it? Do you feel like your energy has been drained? Witchcraft is a deceptive enemy to purpose that we must rid ourselves of completely. Start by asking God to expose all forms of witchcraft in your life. Make it a continuous prayer, and I believe that God will show you. Make sure when He exposes it, you make a conscious decision to let it go. I'm praying for you, Sis.

Self-Control & Health

This form of distraction may come as a surprise, but I have found that our health and self-control can be sneaky distractions as well. The Bible is very clear about the fact that as believers, we need to fast and take care of our bodies (or should I say the temple of the Holy Spirit). 1 Corinthians 6:19-20 says, *"Or do you not know that your body is a temple of the Holy Spirit within you, whom you have from God? You are not your own, for you were bought with a price. So glorify God in your body."* We are not glorifying God with our bodies when we are overweight due to a lack of self-control and discipline. This is so important because if we are operating in self-destruction mode due to the way we treat our bodies, we won't be here to fulfill the purpose God has for our lives. God desires that we live long, healthy lives. I can recall moments when I found myself concerned about my weight, only to realize that it was because I had lost control of my eating. As I came to this realization concerning my eating, God began to expose to me the "why" behind my eating. I can admit that I have indulged in "comfort foods" when I've been emotionally stressed out. I have felt so in love with food that I have eaten without any restraint because it pleased my appetite. Isn't that ironic? Many times we eat the very things that cause us to feel unhealthy because they taste or make us "feel" good. Go watch a few episodes of My 600-lb Life and you'll see exactly what I'm talking about. It seems as though sometimes we struggle to have the willpower to say "No". When I mention eating, I'm not talking about the occasional overindulgence on holidays or special events. I'm talking about knowing we need to change our daily habits but not having the power within to push the plate back or deny certain foods.

Did you know that studies have shown that sugar is just as addictive as cocaine? It provides a short-term high and sends energy through the body, which is exactly the experience of someone who uses drugs. Let me go ahead and testify to this one to make you feel less alone and more empowered to change. I have to frequently take breaks from sugar because I will start to feel like I "need" it. It's like I literally can't say no. This temptation still creeps in when I am not mindful of what I allow my flesh to indulge in. This is where fasting is an invaluable component of our journeys. Fasting has so many health benefits, but it also teaches us the valuable lesson of telling ourselves no. Fasting pushes us to learn how to deny ourselves, which is important because always saying yes to ourselves can be dangerous. Fasting also gives us an opportunity to get closer to God. As we deny all the habitual and random temptations to eat, we are able to redirect our thoughts to God. We pray and ask Him to sustain us and give us the strength to say no. We rely on our commitment to Him to keep us going.

Food currently has power over so many people in the world today. 42.4% of American adults are currently overweight. I'm convinced that a lot of that is due to a lack of self-control. I've often seen in the church how gluttony is accepted and overlooked. Mention fasting to some of the most spiritual people, and they will laugh at you in amazement of your desire to push back the plate. I know this to be true because I was one of them. I even had the nerve to think fasting wasn't necessary because I was focused on more "serious sins". I didn't realize how dependent I was on the satisfaction of food or how in times of stress, boredom, overwhelm, and loneliness I turned to food instead of praying and reading my word. Fasting can be hard. Sis, I know. But, the way you hear from God and learn to rely on Him while fasting will blow your mind.

I will include two amazing books about fasting written by Ted Shuttlesworth in the reference section in the back of this book. These books helped me recognize the spiritual and physical benefits of fasting. After reading *The Complete Guide to Biblical Fasting*, I knew that God wanted me to prepare for warfare. He wants the same for you, so don't follow my lead and wait until you're ten years into your spiritual journey to make fasting a part of your spiritual arsenal. You should consider fasting to be one of your big guns. Pull it out when you know there's something you need to hear clearly from God. While writing this book, God called me to a 7-day absolute fast. Yes, water only, Sis. Girl, I'm not gonna lie; I thought it was Satan talking to me, but after feeling the nudge for a few days, I was obedient to the voice of God. The first three days I tried and failed. I would start the morning, and before the day was over, I was eating. I cried because I felt so bad that I was allowing my flesh to sabotage me. I called my friend and told her about how I was failing (she fasts consistently), and she said she'd been struggling with the same thing. She agreed to join me on the fast, and for the remaining seven days, we persisted.

We woke up every morning at 5 am and prayed together. We shared the things that were on our hearts and prayed about them. We asked God to strengthen us each day and by the grace of God, we made it. Denying the flesh was not easy, but it was worth every hunger pain. During this time of fasting, God showed me many things about myself and how he wanted to use me for his glory. He showed me how to rely on the Holy Spirit and to see things spiritually. I came out of that fast excited to walk in the authority of God. Even now, there are times where my flesh is not super excited to fast (because I mean, what if Crumbl Cookies comes out with the fire this week), but my spirit is excited because it knows just how necessary fasting is. I used to feel sad when I knew God was calling me to fast because I enjoyed the satisfaction that food gave me. I had to ask myself, is food really that serious? Am I really so emotionally tied to food that the thought of missing it a few days gets me down emotionally? The answer was yes!

I have a friend who has actually done 21 days with no food at all. She was on a mission to provoke God's favor. I aspire to be like her, and I'm thankful to have living examples of discipline in my life. She actually bought me a book about fasting that made me take the discipline more seriously. I guess she knew what I was missing by not fasting. I can now see that I was proud to think that I could figure life out apart from prayer and fasting. Trust me when I tell you that your girl has been humbled! Through the humbling, I was able to recognize just how much I needed to rely on God. One of the things God showed me is that not eating makes the body weak and is a reminder that we are mere humans. If we are expecting God to do supernatural things, we must be clear that it is HIS supernatural power working through us, and not our own. 2 Corinthians 12:8-10 tells us that His strength is made perfect in our weakness. God needs us to know that feeling weak when all hell comes against us is the perfect opportunity for Him to take over and show His power. So, if you have been trying to get over something that seems impossible, FAST. Yield yourself to God by becoming weak and relying on Him. God is sure to show up on your behalf.

Sis, give it a try. Start fasting from 6 am to 6 pm one day a week. Then try one day with no food at all. After that, try three days with no food at all and just keep working your way up. Tim Shuttlesworth once said, "There will never be a convenient time to fast, you have to dedicate your time to the Lord". It's so true! Usually, the first day I decide to fast someone brings chocolate cake or donuts to work, and my flesh considers moving the fast to the next day. I now know that temptation is just the enemy's attempt to get me to allow my flesh to win over my spirit. Aht Aht, we are not doing that! So go for it, you can do it, Girl!

Sororities (The Divine 9)

Where I was raised, you either wanted to join the Delta Sigma Theta or Alpha Kappa Alpha (AKA) Sorority. I grew up wanting to be a Delta. Deltas were known for being down-to-earth, popular, and chill. AKA's were known as the pretty, sophisticated, uppity girls that most of us wanted to be, but weren't sure we'd make the cut. I personally felt Delta fit me better because they didn't seem to care much about looks and social status, the very things I had none of at the time. When I joined the military right out of high school, those options were no longer available to me, but I was quickly told about the benefits of being an Eastern Star. Eastern Stars were like the sister organization of the Freemasons. Many of the black leaders in the Army were proud of their affiliation with freemasonry. They would even boast about being favored for promotions and positions because of their membership. Around this time is when my eyes were being opened to the spiritual aspects of things like sororities and fraternities.

I started researching how and why Christians shouldn't join these organizations, and I was quickly convinced that these things weren't for me. I'd watched my aunt fall on hard times, and when she was no longer able to pay her membership dues, she was cut off from the "sisterhood". I think this sisterhood abandonment damaged her self-esteem because a large part of her confidence came from being a member of the highly esteemed AKA. When she couldn't live up to the image that the sorority portrayed, she got down on herself and became very ashamed of where she was in life. My sister wanted desperately to become an AKA but was repeatedly rejected. She felt like becoming an AKA would boost her self-esteem and make her feel accepted. On the other hand, I didn't like the idea of needing something like that to feel successful. If the sisterhood wasn't going to help me when I needed it most, what was the point of a conditional sisterhood?

What really sealed the deal for me was the moment I asked my dad about denouncing his Freemason membership. I remember him saying, "Once a member, always be a member". He didn't seem happy about it, but instead, he sounded as though he was trapped. He believed in his heart that there was no turning back or being set free. I tried reminding him that *whom the Son sets free is free indeed (John 8:36)*, but he was convinced that this membership was irrevocable. I felt helpless at that time because I wasn't equipped to really minister deliverance to my father.

I was just figuring it all out myself. I am still praying for an opportunity to help him receive God's deliverance, and I believe God will honor my prayer in the near future. I shared those experiences with you because I too felt drawn to these organizations before God opened my eyes to the ways they separate us and cause us to glorify self. If this is your first time hearing that these organizations hinder your walk with God, consider your own experience and ask God to show you the truth. If you are sure that there's no demonic spiritual implications, then genuinely asking God to reveal His truth should come without hesitation. I ask that you consider the pledge at the end of the initiation ritual and the following scripture that describes how

God feels about us pledging our affection, heart, mind, and strength to a false god.

> *"To thee, O Alpha Kappa Alpha!*
>
> *We pledge our hearts, our minds, our strength:*
>
> *To foster their teachings,*
>
> *Obey thy laws,*
>
> *And make thee Supreme in Service to all mankind*
>
> *O, Alpha Kappa Alpha, We greet thee!*

> **Exodus 20:3-5 (NLT)**
>
> *3 "You must not have any other god but me. 4 "You must not make for yourself an idol of any kind or an image of anything in the heavens or on the earth or in the sea. 5 You must not bow down to them or worship them, for I, the Lord your God, am a jealous God who will not tolerate your affection for any other gods.*

If you've been through these initiation rituals/ceremonies, then you know more than I do. I trust that God will show you the truth based on your heart condition. He loves you and wants to set you free. There are several testimonies across the internet of people who have denounced, so it may be helpful to hear the perspective of people who have shared in your experience. It is simply my job to bring to your awareness the possibility of a demonic influence unknowingly operating in your life. Most people have no idea that pledging our affections to these organizations is this deep. Ask God to show you, and he will lead you on the right path of denunciation so that you can glorify your Father in Heaven and not an organization. God has already given you His stamp of approval, and that is enough to open doors for which no man on earth could ever take credit. As you seek Him on a deeper level, He will add exactly what you need to your life at the appropriate time (Matthew 6:33). I'm praying for you, Sis.

Friends

Finally, we are here at the one thing that often seems to be the hardest to navigate when we start getting serious about God: friendships. Yes, girl, your friendships. Friends have the potential to propel you into your purpose or to keep you stagnant. It's often unintentional, but nevertheless, stagnation still occurs when we refuse to let go of friendships that are not headed in the same direction. I don't agree with the "cut everybody off" mantra, but I do think establishing boundaries in friendship is critical when we are trying to get serious about growing in God. I remember being so lonely at the beginning of my process of trying to change for the better. I wasn't feeling the parties anymore, but I thought that hanging out with church people would be boring. I remember attending a church picnic, and someone called me. I was cursing so much on the phone, and didn't even realize how natural it was for me. I now know that seeing my behavior around other Christians was the first step in recognizing that I had work to do. Being in a new environment where people expressed themselves without cursing was new for me, but being in those environments made me recognize the need to do better.

I'm sure they thought I was wild (I somewhat was), but they kept encouraging me. I kept showing up to church and eventually made friends who quickly became sisters. I was tired of living in the same cycles, so I figured that church could help me figure my life out. And trust me, there are levels to this thing. While I had gotten a portion of revelation and transformation, there were still so many things God would continue showing me later. I'm no longer the friend that you call to share details about one night stands or how much you hate your husband. Instead, my friends come to me because they can trust that I'm going to empathize and encourage them to get through it in a way that pleases God. I haven't always been that friend though. I've been the friend in the amen corner with no concern for whether or not it pleased God. However, my position toward friendship changed because of how much the older women in my life encouraged me to fight in a Godly way. They taught me to let God fight for me even when I preferred other methods. They called me higher, and I'm so glad they did because it taught me how to call my own friends higher.

There were also times when friends didn't understand my commitment to change. They'd say things like, "if you're really my friend, you'll come with me to the club". I fell for that one time and I was uncomfortable the whole night. I was in there asking people the last time they went to church and then inviting them. Girl, they never asked me to come again. I also got into the habit of telling my friends that if they couldn't respect where I was in my walk with God, then maybe we weren't really friends. It took courage, but I was proud of myself for setting that boundary. I had no hard feelings about them living life as they saw fit, but I was no longer participating and I meant that. I don't think they were on an intentional mission to draw me away from God, but I understood that boundaries needed to be set so I wouldn't end up desiring worldly things again.

I know that sometimes we want to believe that having close relationships with people who habitually do things that don't please God is harmless, but that is not the case. God's word warns us in Matthew 15:33, *"Be not deceived: bad company corrupts good morals"*. The fact that He tells us not to be *deceived* lets me know that the corruption process can be sneaky. If you find yourself going backward in your spiritual growth after connecting with someone, you may need to get real about setting some boundaries. If you feel your energy being drained, or you find yourself continuously talking someone off the ledge, maybe you need to consider the role you play in their life. This is different from a friend going through a rough season, because we all have those. I'm talking about people who continuously put themselves in toxic situations and refuse to make any real attempts to change. You can provide sound advice, and yet they ignore it and come back to dump all their burdens on you time after time. This, my friend, is not a healthy friendship. Love this person, but do yourself a favor and limit how much access you give them. There is no way to completely avoid conflict in all relationships, but we have to know the difference between having a challenging season and having a drama-filled lifestyle.

Listen, this principle even goes for family members. There are some family members who have no intention of asking for or taking your advice. They simply want to fill you in on the latest drama that you can do nothing about. They just want to gossip. I have learned how to preserve my spirit and I no longer take certain phone calls first thing in the morning or at times when I feel a bit overwhelmed myself. I noticed that there are those who often don't even ask how I'm doing or if I'm in the right mental space to take on drama that I can't do anything about. I even catch myself forgetting to consider sometimes. I now realize how important it is to stop and genuinely ask my friend how they are doing before sharing anything that's heavy. I am sure to do this because I can remember getting phone calls that went right into drama, without consideration for what I was going through mentally, spiritually, or physically. I would be listening to their problems so upset because I was dealing with my own problems, but I didn't know how to advocate for myself. Hearing so much negativity was not good for my spirit, especially because I'm naturally a fixer.

Guarding your spirit can be super hard if you are considered "the strong friend". I had to have uncomfortable conversations and tell my friends to ask how I was doing before dumping on me. As women, we are wired to talk and share our feelings to feel better. In an effort to unload, we sometimes don't consider how the receiver feels at the time of our dump. This is no reason to end a friendship because we are often just repeating what we've seen our whole lives, but it is an opportunity for a boundary-setting conversation. This is a great opportunity to practice healthy conflict by advocating for yourself in uncomfortable situations. Sure, your friend may feel like you're calling them a negative Nancy, but what if they really are? What if you really are? Listen, we all have moments where we need to vent, blow off some steam, or want someone to understand our point of view. Learning to navigate how and when to do that is a part of any relationship. When we set boundaries and express how others affect us, it gives them a chance to make things better. Of course, it would be way easier to just cut a friend off, but you will eventually cut off all human connections in exchange for loneliness. Friendships take work, but when we set boundaries and communicate what we need, they can be very rewarding.

So have your friendships, Sis. Choose the close ones wisely. Quality friendships require patience, forgiveness, and love. Some of us have not had the best examples of friendships and have sometimes been hurt by someone you considered a close friend. Don't allow a bad experience (or a poor choice in past friends) to stop you from receiving new friends into your life. When we eliminate friendships from our life due to past hurt, we miss out on so much. The thing I value most about a good friendship is having someone that can give me honest counsel in tough times, because sometimes we just don't know the answer. *Proverbs 27:9 (NIV) says "Oil and perfume make the heart glad; So does the sweetness of a friend's counsel that comes from the heart".* I try to maintain close friendships that will not only agree with me but also keep it real and give me advice from the heart. You'll know whether you can trust these friends based on the life they live and how they show up for you, themselves, and others.

Discouragement

There will be moments on this journey that will straight up discourage you. There will be times when you will pray and feel like God isn't hearing you. As you start to desire the things of God, you may feel lonely. You'll be excited to change, but quickly realize that not everyone is on the same page. If you're not careful, those feelings of loneliness will make you question whether getting serious about God was the right decision. I want you to be encouraged that we all go through these natural feelings of discouragement when trying to do something new. Think about it. You've been doing things your way for a long time and this new method requires you to depend on a source other than yourself. Discouragement is defined as having lost confidence or enthusiasm. I know it's hard to keep doing something when you don't see results, but I want to remind you that doing so is the epitome of faith. Hebrews 11:1 (NKJV) says, *"Now faith is the [a]substance of things hoped for, the [b]evidence of things not seen"*.

That means that we must continue to believe something will happen even when our reality doesn't reflect it. I know, it sounds crazy to think that your spouse can be delivered when reality shows that they have no desire for God. You sometimes feel foolish believing that God will heal you from a sickness or improve your financial situation when there is no physical manifestation. I believe that one of the enemy's greatest tactics of discouragement is to tempt us to focus on the ways that our realities do not match the promises of God. If he can get us to lean on and trust in our realities, we will remain discouraged. He loves to see us wavering between belief in God and belief in what we see around us. Trust me, I've been there. I would leave church motivated and inspired, only to get home and face the fact that nothing has changed in the natural realm. Instantly, feelings of discouragement and doubt would overwhelm me, making me feel like believing in God for something different was pointless. Thankfully, I now understand that this is a common strategy used by Satan to get Christians to remain double-minded. James 1:6-8 warns us that we won't get anything from God being that way.

> *But when you ask, you must believe and not doubt, because the one who doubts is like a wave of the sea, blown and tossed by the wind. That person should not*

expect to receive anything from the Lord. Such a person is double-minded and unstable in all they do.
James 1:6-8 (NIV)

What if our double-mindedness is the reason we stay in seasons of not seeing God answer prayers? What if He's waiting on us to truly believe what we're asking for? I know that regardless of how much faith we have, God still moves when He sees fit. All I'm saying is that we need to make sure we're not the reason for our own seasons of prolonged suffering.

I have used a lot of marriage examples in this book because nothing has tested my faith like marriage. I have been believing God to do some things in my husband for a really long time, but I must admit that I have been double-minded at times. I have noticed that when I approach God with confidence for these positive changes in my husband (things that align with God's Word), I'm not as easily discouraged. Sometimes, I see the total opposite, but that doesn't change the fact that I know God is capable of working on my husband's behalf. I try to keep in mind that the enemy would love for me to give up on him, my family, and even some friends. I refuse to do that.

Sometimes, there are people who don't have the courage to believe for positive change, but our faith can inspire them that there is still hope. This same kind of faith should be applied to our own situations. We must believe that God can change, heal, or forgive without doubt. I've often had to remind myself that there's nothing that God cannot do. So, if He has not answered a prayer, it is for a good reason. We have to grow to trust that He knows best, even when we'd rather Him move our way and on our schedule. Be encouraged, Sis. Moments of discouragement will come, but don't allow yourself to doubt God. Consider whether your thoughts are leading you to believe what Satan is presenting or to embrace God's truth.

Satan has been exposed...

It takes most of us a really long time to recognize some of the distractions mentioned in this chapter. Do not forget that there is a spiritual battle going on for our souls and minds. If Satan can get us to indulge in distractions, he can then keep us bound in repetitive cycles of struggle, stress, addiction, and defeat. We have a real enemy that is jealous of our opportunity to join God in Heaven for eternity. Satan's fate has already been determined, so he is now on a mission to disqualify us from eternity with God. He wants us to join him in Hell, but we will not be doing that! Satan has been on the Earth since he was thrown out of heaven, so he's had the chance to study people for thousands of years. That's why he and his angels are able to strategically attack us without us knowing at times. He uses people, circumstances, and our own desires to get us off track with God. So we must be aware of his schemes, so we don't continue falling for the same tactics. 2 Corinthians 2:11 (NLT) says, *"so that Satan will not outsmart us. For we are familiar with his evil schemes".* Yes, this is an attempt to make you more familiar with his schemes. I've exposed some of the common areas he deceives us so that you can evaluate and make sure that you are not walking in deception.

    A good way to determine if we are really walking with God is to evaluate the fruit in our lives. Galatians makes the works of the flesh very clear in chapter 5, verses 19-21:

> *When you follow the desires of your sinful nature, the results are very clear: sexual immorality, impurity, lustful pleasures, [20] idolatry, sorcery, hostility, quarreling, jealousy, outbursts of anger, selfish ambition, dissension, division, [21]envy, drunkenness, wild parties, and other sins like these. Let me tell you again, as I have before, that anyone living that sort of*

life will not inherit the Kingdom of God. **Genesis 5:19-21 (NLT)**

If we are living according to our flesh, some of these things will be present in our lives. These things prevent us from walking in obedience to God and truly experiencing the blessings of God. So, take a moment to be real with yourself. If you see yourself operating in any of these things, I urge you to ask God to help you let them go. There's no shame here because God wants you to acknowledge your error, ask for forgiveness, and make a conscious effort to do things differently. Unfortunately, many Christians know that they are walking in error but refuse to change because it often means sacrificing their own desires for the things of God. In their minds, they can't imagine giving up sex, parties, liquor, or a sorority because they have not asked God to change their desires to fall into alignment with His. When He changes our desires, we will come to mourn the days we followed the desires that only wanted to destroy us.

"Why do demons wish to excite in us gluttony, fornication, greed, anger, rancor and other passions? So that the mind, under their weight, should be unable

to pray as it ought; for when the passions of our irrational part begin to act, they prevent the mind from acting rationally." ~ St. Nilus of Sinai

The enemy has a strong desire to keep you bound to the things of the world without any conviction that they are not pleasing to God. The enemy knows that if we begin to feel comfortable in sin, we're less likely to let it go. After all, everyone else is doing it, so it can't be that bad or that serious. Sis, remember that you are not everyone else. You and lukewarm Christians are not the same! Living for God means doing what everyone else is NOT doing. Matthew 7:13-14 says 13 *"You can enter God's Kingdom only through the narrow gate. The highway to hell[a] is broad, and its gate is wide for the many who choose that way. 14 But the gateway to life is very narrow and the road is difficult, and only a few ever find it".* Therefore, the goal should be to stay off the highway to hell. I'm on a mission to let go of anything hindering my walk with God. That includes things, people, behaviors, places, and attitudes. If, like me, you are determined to grow in your relationship with God, now is a good time to make the confession again... God, I'm serious this time. Only this time, you should really mean it.

Let's Pray.

Lord, thank you for opening my eyes to all the ways Satan has been deceiving me and others. Thank you for showing me the things that may be preventing me from serving you wholeheartedly. Forgive me for putting these things before you. Take away my desire for the things that don't please you. I want to love what you love and hate what you hate. Help me to be more like you, God. Help me to share this knowledge with others in love. Help me to extend grace to those walking in error and draw them to your truth with love. Don't let me forget how dirty I was and how you still loved me. Help me to remember those low moments when I want to become prideful. Use me as a vessel to help snatch others out of the same darkness I once found myself in. Help me to be patient and long-suffering, knowing that only you can truly change someone. I rebuke any curses that have been spoken over my life. Thank you that the blood of Christ has cleansed me from all unrighteousness and that no weapon, curse, or spell formed against me will ever prosper because I belong to God. I denounce any affiliation with zodiac signs or horoscopes. I no longer identify with the character of zodiac signs, but I take on the mind and character of Christ. Give me the character and personality that you assigned to me in my mother's womb. Help me to be less concerned about social media and more about living my real life for you. I no longer want to be hindered by any of these things, Lord. Help me to live for you and not for my flesh. Give me the wisdom to know what is pleasing to you and what is not. In Jesus Name, Amen

Chapter 6

What is a Godly Woman ?

Favor is deceitful, and beauty is vain: but a woman that feareth the LORD, she shall be praised.
Proverbs 31:30

What do "They" Say a Good Woman Is?

Everyone has an opinion about what a "good woman" is, but does God agree with those opinions? There are men who think that a good woman is a lady in the streets and a freak in the sheets. Ok, I may have just told you how old I'm getting with that statement, but I know y'all have heard that theory before. There are some who think a good woman is one who cooks, cleans, has a sexy body, and is submissive to her man. In fact, most men expect to experience all these qualities in a woman before she becomes his wife. She's expected to perform sexually and demonstrate her potential to be independent yet submissive. Some definitions of a good woman imply that women are expected to be more like mothers to men versus their potential help-meets. The previous opinions are just a few things I've heard men say and some of my past personal expectations for what it meant to be a good woman.

Let me just say that I've tried to live up to most of these expectations, and it only left me feeling used and further away from the goal of becoming a good woman. I often gave too much and received very little in return due to my lack of clarity on what it actually meant to be a good woman. Like many women, my focus was on what "men" considered to be a good woman. I was striving to be acceptable in the eyes of men instead of in the eyes of God. The issue with striving to be good in the eyes of men is that every man wants something different, and most of those desires are shaped by their personal experiences with other women. Their mothers, the media, and its unrealistic expectations have created a standard that often isn't realistic. In other words, we may never be good enough if we change depending on who we're dating or trying to attract.

Society and culture also have their opinions about what it means to be a good woman. The most common opinion that I see is the image of a college-educated, boss mentality, with a sexy physique, and a provocative woman who wants, but does not need a man. We are highly encouraged through many sources to walk in our "masculine energy," which means to take on masculine characteristics like being assertive, independent, competitive, tough, and driven. While these are good qualities to have, too much of them can lead us to lay down our feminine qualities if we are not careful. God gave us our feminine qualities for a purpose, but life experiences can stop us from feeling comfortable operating in those areas of our nature. For example, if my kindness was always taken as a weakness, I may take on a more dominant attitude when dealing with people to avoid being seen as weak. In my own life, I personally found myself struggling to turn off the dominant attitude when dealing with my husband, which put a strain on our relationship and was not pleasing to God. This attitude of dominance was beneficial for my career but ineffective for my marriage. I now know that I often took charge and asserted myself out of fear, the need for control, and to avoid being let down. For a while, I thought this mindset was working for me, but I quickly found that trying to control everything and everyone gets tiring and is impossible. As we seek true healing, we can learn to trust God with people and circumstances instead of relying on our power and ability.

When we attempt to follow society's recommendations for a good woman, we have to ensure that we don't allow it to consume and overwhelm us with mental, emotional, and physical stress. While some women are capable of chasing, acquiring, and maintaining the independent boss status, that life is not for everyone. You are not less of a woman because you don't have a degree or a six-figure salary. So, if you have been believing that lie and running yourself ragged to achieve the world's idea of success, let this be your sign to release that narrative. The truth is that God doesn't place a lot of value on those things. No disrespect to the women who choose that path, but I've found that they too eventually realize the need for spiritual fulfillment that can only be achieved through Christ. So while men, other women, and society have made their expectations clear, it's time to see what the Creator has to say about womanhood.

God's Definition of a Good Woman

I'm so glad that God's definition is not like the world's. God isn't concerned about our degrees, titles, salaries, body shapes, or the cars that we drive. God's definition of a good woman is a Godly woman. I'm not just talking about a woman who goes to church consistently and has the physical appearance of a godly woman. I'm referring to the woman who lives publicly and privately as though she is guided by the Holy Spirit. She considers God in all her ways and is more concerned with her God-given purpose than the expectations of others. When looking for an image of a godly woman, most people head straight to Proverbs 31 to get it, but the

Proverbs 31 woman isn't the only example of godliness that God has given us in His Word. Not every woman has a family or is in preparation for one. In fact, some women get discouraged reading about the Proverbs 31 woman because she was clearly conquering womanhood, motherhood, and being a wife in a way that seems unattainable.

Take a few moments to pause from reading the book and go read the entire chapter of Proverbs 31, even if you've read it a thousand times. While our Proverbs 31 sister had it together, do not be discouraged because there are also women in the Bible who had a rocky start in life but eventually found their way to God. God included the Proverbs 31 example in the Bible to inspire us, not to discourage us. When I read how the Proverbs 31 woman handled life, it gives me something to strive toward as a woman, wife, and mother. In this chapter, King Lemuel's mom wanted the best for her son, so she gave him qualities to help identify a woman with good character. Before exploring all the qualities of this woman, she warns him. She starts by telling him that this type of woman is hard to find, and she was not lying. But why? Why is this type of woman hard to find when so many women claim to be Christians? Most of her characteristics are based on biblical principles. I think the answer is life. Living life in a fallen world makes it challenging to walk in all of these qualities. Some of us have not had examples of Godly women to learn from. We are often influenced from a very young age to imitate that which we see in popular art and music, which often doesn't provide biblical examples. That's why it is so important to consider the foundation that our idea of womanhood was built on. What were you eager to experience in womanhood? I was most excited to party, get myself a man, and have kids. Fearing the Lord was the furthest thing from my mind.

    Let's talk about fearing the Lord. Do you fear Him? Not in a scary way, but in a way that is reverential? Do you desire to please God with your life? Look at it this way: when you fear losing your job, you try to follow all the rules. When you love your job, you also put your best foot forward to maintain your employment. Your objective is to be a great employee and follow the instructions of the one who hired you. You don't attempt to change the rules that you don't agree with because you understand that you are not the owner of the organization. Your overall goal at work is to please those who hired you. If we take on a similar perspective with God, it may help us revere His position in our lives with greater intention. However, this reverence doesn't always come naturally. God instructs parents to train up children in the way they should go according to God's word, but that's often not the case. We are told to follow our hearts, do what "feels" right, and to embrace other cultural cliches instead of God. There are parents who don't spend a lot of time encouraging a relationship with God, which encourages us to please our parents, not God. When we spend the majority of our life trying to please ourselves and other people, we can go down paths that do not lead to God's intended purpose and will for our lives. When we don't learn about God from a young age, we end up taking on the character of those who have the greatest influence on us. Yeah, I went to church every Sunday as a young girl, but it was a formality. Sure, I kept "some" of the commandments in mind, but I didn't really have a relationship with God for myself. I was more focused on not getting caught by my mom than honoring God. I was more concerned with being liked by my friends than I was about being liked by God. God was more of a Sunday thing, not a lifestyle, and I didn't yet understand what I was missing.

So again, how was your character shaped? How are you as a person? Have you asked God to start shaping you into a better woman inside and out? Do you even think there's a need for change? News flash, if you don't see a need for change, you may be walking in pride. When we start to acknowledge our need for help, God can come in and help us. Matthew 7:7 says, *"Ask and it will be given to you; seek and you will find; knock and the door will be opened to you."* I have to remind myself that if I'm not getting the answers that I need, I may be asking the wrong source or looking to the wrong places for inspiration. I literally beg God to help me and show me how to overcome the things preventing me from walking in His complete will for my life. His answer isn't always what I want to hear, but it's necessary if I'm going to grow. So, be real with and about yourself. I'm telling you, Sis. When you start to take ownership of your need to change, God will show you the areas to work on. The objective isn't to make you into a perfect person. The goal is to help you to heal the areas that sabotage your efforts to love, receive love, and grow. In the midst of this growth, you'll start to desire the qualities of a Godly woman. The following passage gives us insight into the qualities of good Christian women:

> *Older women similarly are to be reverent in their behavior, not malicious gossips nor addicted to much wine, teaching what is right and good, 4 so that they may encourage the young women to tenderly love their husbands and their children, 5 to be sensible, pure, makers of a home [where God is honored], good-natured, being subject to their own husbands, so that the word of God will not be dishonored.* **Titus 2:3-5 (NASB)**

Let's break this passage down a little further. The scripture starts out talking about how older women should carry themselves. This principle is important because we should be learning how to be good women from those who have been doing this thing longer than we have. It is my personal expectation for teen girls and young adult women to be able to learn from me by watching my actions as a woman, wife, and mother. I try to surround myself with older women who can pour into me and teach me how to navigate aging with wisdom and grace.

However, I've learned that age is not a guarantee that someone is wise or reverent in their walk with God. We can easily identify women who carry themselves with grace in how they speak and treat others. It's almost as though you can physically see the peace that they have learned to exude from walking with God. They have a confidence that seems unshakable, but upon talking to them, they will tell you how they withstood many tests and trials that made their faith stronger over the years. Reverent women carry themselves with respect for God and themselves. They are careful not to misrepresent God in how they navigate life. They have allowed God to transform their mind, and they embrace the blessing of aging.

Take a moment to think about how you currently show up. Who would people say you belong to? Is it evident that God is a part of your life? How do you treat people? Are you harsh or gentle? Loving or argumentative? Does your public life match your private life?

I believe that Paul instructs us to get our behavior under control first for a reason. This isn't done by forcing ourselves to behave differently just for the sake of it, but it comes from getting to know what God expects of us and praying for Him to make His priorities ours. As we begin to love what God loves and hate what He hates, our behavior will begin to change as we discipline ourselves and commit to God and His ways.

Drunken Gossips

One thing about women, if we are not intentional, we will almost always find ourselves gossiping! Webster defines gossip as casual or unconstrained conversation about other people, usually involving details that are not confirmed as true. Let me be the first to say, this has been me, and is me if I am not careful. Gossip seems innocent, but in reality, it can destroy families, friendships, relationships, and even work environments. Some of us grew up seeing everyone getting along at gatherings, but before everyone left, the gossip had already begun. This was so deceptive because the individual being talked about had no way to defend themselves, and the people talking were convinced their information was accurate. Seeing this type of behavior often made me question whether people's words were genuine any time people said or did nice things for me. As children, we were taught how to act nice but talk about the unconfirmed business of people who were no longer in our presence. I honestly never really thought twice about gossip being wrong; after all, I wasn't saying it to their face or damaging the other party in any way. Surely, harmless gossiping with my closest friends was acceptable, right? Nope. There was a time in my life where gossip felt safe and I felt no need for self-restraint. I could say whatever I wanted to knowing that it wouldn't get beyond the sphere of my inner circle.

This type of gossip is also deceptive because as Christians, we often end up talking about people with no intention to pray for them. At least that's how it was for me. Gossip starts out being with those closest to you, but it eventually seeps over into other areas of your life. People would tell me stuff (the tea) at work, and I would share it with a friend. Before you knew it, I was being called in to confirm the things I had said in private. Being caught up in this way was embarrassing. I started to notice how I was always in drama and mess. I thought gossip was harmless, but it was causing problems for myself and the people I was talking about. And guess what, it was almost always unconfirmed information. I know, just messy! It took some time, but I eventually caught on to the deceptive nature of gossip.

Now, before you assume that I'm saying everything you discuss about another person is considered gossip, let me be clear. Sometimes, people will bring up another person in order to get advice on navigating difficult situations. In those times, we have to use wisdom to discern how to best help the person make sense of what has happened. The goal should always be reconciliation. God wants us to be peacemakers, meaning we are to help bring reconciliation. I try to do this by remaining neutral when the other party is not present, regardless of who I'm talking to. When people start gossiping or talking negatively, I interject with possible perspectives of the other person that caused the offense. This type of regulation makes it clear that I am not taking sides without being privy to all of the details. The goal when engaged in conflict resolution with others is to make sure I can feel comfortable repeating myself when both parties are present. This keeps me honest. I've come to the conclusion that most people will stop trying to turn you against the person when you do not agree with everything they say.

It's a lot, but Paul was well aware of our nature as women when he instructed us to avoid malicious gossip. Malicious means to do something with an intent to harm another person's character, reputation, or physical well-being. Let's be real... little girls and teenagers are not the only ones who can be malicious when talking about people. I remember maliciously talking about other women that I was jealous of. I was insecure, and talking about another woman somehow made me feel better about myself. The goal was to bring her down because I was too insecure to appreciate someone that I perceived was doing better than I was. At the root of gossip is often a poor heart condition. Now that I'm healed, I don't desire to talk about women in that way. It took work, but I had to ask God to help me really like myself. Now that I like myself, the good qualities of others don't make me feel inferior. So yeah, if you find yourself instantly being negative toward others, it may be an indication that you have some insecurities to work through. Gossip may seem to make you feel better than the person you're speaking negatively about, but it will only feel good temporarily. Sooner or later, you will be faced with the same insecurities you tried to cover up by putting someone else down. It's time to work through those issues, Sis. Take a moment to consider the areas you always find yourself gossiping about others, whether that's relationships, finances, past mistakes, poor decisions, appearances, associations, or career choices. If you are insecure in any of these areas, this may be why you find yourself eager to put people down. We've all been there, and the key to freedom is recognizing when you begin to think negatively in your heart about someone. I try to snap out of it quickly and force myself to have compassion. There are so many reasons people may make poor choices or end up in situations that open them up to being gossiped about. Just remember, your sideline chatter is not going to make a difference unless you are given a chance to share your perspective with that person. If we're being honest, most of the time we're not bold enough to say the things we say behind people's backs to their faces. So stop yourself from gossiping and ask God to show the areas within you that need healing.

 Now, let's move on to the "do not be drunken with much wine" part. Isn't it ironic that culture glorifies and normalizes mothers drinking wine often? Every time I turn around, I see media images of some woman living a luxurious life as she pours a glass of wine, as though that is the ultimate sign of relaxation, self-care, or success. It's harmless, they say. Maybe a glass of wine every now and then is harmless, but needing a glass of wine to decompress may not be the healthiest habit to adopt, especially if you have children. Paul says that she must not be given "much" wine, but why? The Bible mentions people drinking wine on several occasions, and it often refers to it in a way that is not beneficial. I'm not here to argue whether drinking is right or wrong, but to simply present reasons why Paul warns us not to overdo it. Ephesians 5:16-18(NIV) says *"making the most of every opportunity, because the days are evil. 17 Therefore do not be foolish, but understand what the Lord's will is. 18 Do not get drunk on wine, which leads to debauchery. Instead, be filled with the Spirit.....".*

Webster defines debauchery as excessive indulgence in sensual pleasures, lack of morals, lack of principles, or lack of restraint. I can personally testify to the truth that alcohol leads to all of these things. I did things drunk that I would have never done sober. We all know the quiet person that can't keep quiet once they've had a few drinks. Yes, I know alcohol doesn't affect everyone the same, but we are warned to not be "drunken" with wine for a reason. Drunken means given to habitual, excessive use of alcohol. You can do with that what you will, but if you have a desire to truly represent God and hear from Him, it is going to require a sober mind. I ask that you pray and ask God what He has to say about you and your heart toward alcohol. Are you using it to calm you down? Does your flesh desire it when you need a sense of joy and peace? Is it used to comfort you in times of loneliness, stress, or overwhelm? If you answered yes to any of these questions, you may be using wine to do what the Holy Spirit desires to do. No shame here, Sis. Repent and ask God to help you desire the Holy Spirit in the times where you would usually lean on alcohol instead. It will be challenging initially, but the more you deny your flesh, the less control it will have over you. You can do it, Sis. With Christ, all things... Yep, you already know the rest (Matthew 19:26).

Teaching what is right & good

There are a lot of women out here teaching things, but are they right and good? As a young woman, it's very important to be cautious about who is teaching you. As older women, God expects us to set a good example for those coming behind us. I remember being a teen, excited about becoming a woman so that I could have the freedom to do what the older women were doing. They were turning up, clubbing, and free to do whatever they wanted. I couldn't wait to do the same thing. It seemed exciting, but I now know that those women were not teaching me what was good and right. They didn't even realize what they were teaching me with their lifestyles.

Good and right teaching comes from the word of God, and not the preferences of those that we look up to. I remember giving horrible advice before getting into a real relationship with God. I even told a friend that she should leave her husband for someone that "I" thought was a better choice for her. When God reminded me of that, I repented and even asked her for forgiveness. I tell you this story because I want you to see how I really thought I was giving solid advice. Thank God my friend had enough sense to ignore my advice because they have been happily married for almost 18 years now. Whew, so make sure you are being taught and are teaching what is good and right according to God. When we accept God's word as truth, we allow it to change us. It shapes the way we see ourselves, others, and our circumstances. We begin to filter our decisions through God's word. His Word then changes the way we choose our friends, music, potential husbands, careers, churches, and organizations.

"But how do I grow in knowing what is good and right?" you're probably asking. It's through the sanctification process. We don't just wake up physically different after accepting Christ. We have to put in work spiritually, mentally, and physically. It will all seem fake initially, but just keep forcing yourself to pray, read God's word, and get around other genuine believers. The more you do Godly stuff, the more you will desire Godly things. This walk with God is self-paced. You determine how fast or slow you go. If you continue doing things that keep you in neutral, expect to stay where you are. When in neutral, you're not going backward, but are you moving forward spiritually? If the answer is no, I want you to consider what you are being intentionally or unintentionally taught. When God reveals an area of your life that needs healing, accept that you need to be taught in that area. If God shows you that you are always trying to please people and make them happy, you must start to listen to trusted sermons about rejection. Find scriptures about rejection. Find scriptures about God's acceptance and love. You have to be determined to learn a new way of thinking about rejection, and God will begin to show you how to overcome it. Good teaching will change your life. I've seen it firsthand.

Tenderly love your husband and children.

Sis, if you are married or have children, you have been entrusted with an area of responsibility that is very important to God. He wants us to be intentional about the role we play in the lives of our husbands and children. Paul says that good women tenderly love their husbands and their children. I thought this principle was pretty obvious, but I guess Paul knew there would be hindrances to us tenderly loving our husbands and children. Tender love goes beyond taking physical care of them. Cooking, buying clothes, and providing shelter are valuable contributions to our households, but they don't necessarily cover the emotional and spiritual aspects of parenting and being a wife. To show tender love means showing kindness, gentleness, and affection. God says love is patient, kind, and keeps no records of wrongs. Some of us may have to pray for God to grow us in the area of tenderly loving our husbands and children. If you find yourself being mean, rough, harsh, and lacking affection, pray for it. Ask God to reveal to you why you find it hard to tenderly love. It could be a form of protection from being hurt. It can also be hard to show affection and gentleness if you were not nurtured that way.

I found it awkward to be seriously affectionate. I would be jokingly affectionate, but it didn't feel natural to do so without joking. I have been getting better in this area, but it is only because I've asked God to help me feel comfortable genuinely expressing love to my husband and children. This love now shows up in random hugs, talking without yelling, and doing things for them without an attitude. How we integrate love into our lifestyle is the best way to teach our children about love. Life, circumstances, trauma, and many other things can hinder us from showing our husbands and kids unconditional love. Keep in mind, God's definition of love is very different from the love heard in songs and cute movies. God's love is patient, kind, and longsuffering. It does not boast. It's not proud, and it doesn't dishonor others. It's not selfish or easily angered and doesn't keep records of wrongs. God's love does not delight in evil but is happy with the truth. It always protects, trusts, hopes, and perseveres.

When we look at love from this perspective, it's easy to see why God needed to remind us to love our husbands and children.

We're all human. God knew we'd have circumstances that would make us consider making our love conditional or removing it altogether. Here is another friendly reminder to love them. I mean like, really love them. Not only does the Bible say that love covers a multitude of sins (1 Peter 4:8), but think about it... Babies, for example, are so easy to love because they have not used their will to intentionally lie, cheat, disobey, or disrespect you. That teenage son or daughter, on the other hand... They have or will be taking you through some challenging moments that will tempt you to love them conditionally if you are not mindful. Because we love our spouses and children so much, it's easy for them to tug at our hearts and souls when things don't go the way we expect, especially when they do something hurtful toward us. Unforgiveness and resentment can creep in and cause us to be nasty and bitter toward them without even realizing it. So take a moment to reflect. Do you tenderly and biblically love your husband and children? What is their experience of you? Do you genuinely talk to them about how they are doing in life? Do you find a way to show them love in difficult seasons? Do you speak to them in a loving way with your tone, body language, and facial expressions? Before considering these questions myself, I felt like as long as their physical needs were met, everything else was me going above and beyond. I honestly didn't care or consider how they were experiencing me as a mom and wife. Since I'm being completely honest, I will admit that my love was very conditional. I have to work extra hard to love in difficult moments. I allow myself the grace to be angry and to process my emotions, but my goal is to not stay there for too long. It's crazy because once I am able to process my emotions and calm down (after removing myself from the environment), God usually gives me more understanding about what happened. In the heat of the moment, the guns are blazing, and the baby and anybody else can get it. So I have learned that if I can't express myself without yelling, it's best to step away and come back when I can talk without being so emotional.

As moms, we have an opportunity to lay the foundation for how our children see the world. We can introduce them to love and acceptance, but if we are not careful, we can also introduce them to hate and rejection. In one season, I was wondering why my son found it hard to stand up for himself at school. God revealed to me that I had been one of his first bullies. He was accustomed to being forced to accept my harsh talk when I got upset. He wasn't given a chance to advocate for himself in difficult moments when he was a child. I'll be honest and say that I often didn't even give him room to express his emotions. Saying things like "Shut up! And Stop Crying!" in moments where speaking up and crying may have been justified. Girl, looking back, I now know that was shaping the confidence he would have when he experienced conflict with other people. At the time, I just considered myself being a firm parent and doing what I knew to work best.

    I didn't see any examples of child and parent conflict resolution growing up. When we saw white parents on television allowing their children to express themselves, it was seen as weak, toxic, and pushover parenting style. I now know SOME of them were teaching their children to advocate for themselves in a safe space, so that they would be capable of doing the same thing when they left home. We often do what we know as moms, until we realize there are other options available to us. When my eyes were opened to my error, it took a lot of effort to control myself and allow my son the freedom to advocate for himself. I had to change my tone and facial expressions, and ask God to help me give him space to evolve without feeling controlled and dominated by me. I am still working on this even as I write this book, so please be encouraged. If you find yourself doing any of these same things, give yourself grace. Remember that your intentions were often pure when parenting, but you just had a lack of knowledge and patience. Now that you recognize some areas that you can soften up and can make a conscious effort to change, tell your children you are sorry for whatever you have done and let them know you are working to change those behaviors. You will be surprised at how receptive they are. This exercise will not only teach them that we all make mistakes, but how to own those mistakes and make a conscious effort to change.

This may also be a good time to reflect on how you developed your parenting style. Think about how you were raised and the impact it had on your life. People often avoid this type of reflection for fear of judging their parents, but please understand that our parents did the best they could. The resources available to you were probably not available back then, so this is not a license to shame them but to forgive them and extend grace to them. By evaluating your childhood from this new perspective, you get to use the data to shift the family dynamics for your children and grandchildren. You are setting your bloodline up for greater success, just like most of our parents tried to do for us. So let's strive to obey God in the area of loving our children and husband.

Self-Controlled and Pure

Sis, we've been talking about some serious topics, but let's continue pushing through, knowing that God has a purpose for us in exploring these areas of our lives. This next topic is no different.

In fact, it may be even more important because self-control gives us the ability to maintain the changes we're making after accepting some truths about where we are in our walk with God. Girl, we can pray all day, but without self-control, we end up repeating the same behaviors and cycles that we desire to change.

Self-control is defined as the ability to regulate one's emotions, thoughts, and behaviors in the face of temptations and impulses. Now, we all know that temptations and impulses are real in all stages of the walk with God. Whether it's resisting the urge to pop off on someone who has wronged you, or using food to cope with emotional issues that God wants to heal, as long as we are in these human bodies, we will have to exercise self-control. We often desire to control other people, but in reality, controlling ourselves is a full-time job. Just imagine who and what you would be without any self-control. In Titus, Paul encourages us to say no to ungodly desires and worldly passions and to live self-controlled, upright, and godly lives in this present age (Titus 2:11-12). He didn't warn us to say no to all of our desires and passions, just the ungodly and worldly ones.

Merriam-Webster defines worldly as relating to, or devoted to this world and its pursuits rather than to religion or spiritual affairs. Sis, that means if all the pursuits that we care about deeply have nothing to do with God or spiritual things, by default, they are worldly. Our desires and passions should involve God and things that are pleasing to Him. It's never too late to start developing Godly desires, but beware that Satan wants us to wait as long as possible to do so. God tells us to seek the kingdom of God first, and he'll add everything else to us (Matthew 6:33). I'm not surprised that the world leads us to chase success, relationships, and thrills before worrying about our spiritual development. In the process of going after our worldly desires and passions, we end up feeling like we're too far gone and attempt to fix ourselves before coming back to God. We often think that we'll magically want to give up our old ways and immediately start having self-control, but things don't usually work that way. Leaving worldly things behind takes God purifying and sanctifying us over time. Transformation is a process that looks different for everyone. Some hearts take longer to open up to God, depending on past experiences and how strong the pull of worldly desires is. Even the writer of the Psalm below is asking how to stay on the path to purity as a young person:

> *9 How can a young person stay on the path of purity? By living according to your word. 10 I seek you with all my heart; do not let me stray from your commands. 11 I have hidden your word in my heart that I might not sin against you.* **Psalm 119:9-11(NIV)**

It's clear that this path to purity is one we must intentionally strive to stay on. The psalmist starts out by saying that he not only reads the word but lives according to it. This shows how easy it is to read the word and then totally forget to apply it to our lives in the heat of the moment. This verse demonstrates how we can quickly neglect what we've read because we haven't hidden it in our hearts, meaning we haven't made God's word the core or foundation of who we are and what we do. The psalmist also mentions how he seeks God with all of his heart. He doesn't say that he is seeking God whenever he has a few extra minutes. He doesn't say that he is seeking God when it's convenient for him or with just a corner of his heart. However, we do see that he is going full out in his pursuit of God. What about you? Can you honestly say you've been seeking God? Are you trying to get to know Him so that He has an opportunity to make you pure?

The psalmist says that he hides God's Word in his heart so that he doesn't sin against it. Biologically, our hearts give life to our entire body. I believe that hiding the word in our hearts allows it to be distributed to all parts of our body. When we commit to hiding the word in our hearts, we go beyond reading a devotional or the scripture of the day. It means seeking out scripture to fit our specific situations. It means reading and studying so that the words really make sense to you. It also means relying on God to help you make sense of it all. When we begin to diligently seek Him, things in our life will start to change. If you have been finding it hard to change some of the behaviors that don't please God, evaluate your pursuit of God. To be impure means contaminated, corrupted, or impregnated with an unclean substance. What impure things are you holding on to? Why do you need to let them go? What would the opposite of that thing look like in your life? If we are going to be good women, we must have a desire to be pure and the willingness to give up the things that prevent us from pursuing purity.

Makers of a Home & Good Natured

A homemaker is someone who manages the affairs of the home. I can say firsthand that there have been seasons when I've been a maker of everything except my home. I was killing it at work and at church, but my own home was in shambles. I spent time cleaning the church and volunteering for work events, with no concern for how those obligations would impact my family. I found myself being super busy in other areas because those things brought me a sense of purpose and validation that cleaning up after my family didn't offer at the time. I could clean the whole house, cook a full meal, restock all the necessities, and not receive one thank you. I think we can all attest to the fact that homemaking can be a thankless job at times. Let me be clear, it is still very thankless at times, but my perspective has changed. While there are so many opportunities to make an impact outside our home, God wants us to value the work we do as women in our home. I think we can all agree that being good-natured while taking care of our homes, our children, and husbands is not always easy. Being good-natured means to be naturally friendly and not get angry easily, and I have to literally put myself in a chokehold to walk this one out. I feel like my tongue should be missing as much as I have had to bite it at times.

    For example, I walked into the house today to clothes on the floor, the trash not taken out, and the laundry unwashed. I had imagined coming home to a semi-clean house since my husband had the day off to himself. The first thought was to send him a video of the stuff he obviously didn't see, but then I calmed down because he went the extra mile and made the bed. Nothing to you, but progress for us lol. My man could have dirty clothes up to the ceiling and see no issues, but he has really been making an effort to help out more, which prompts me to calm down. This may seem like a minuscule example of working on being good-natured, but Sis, it was way worse before intentionally trying to change. My attitude would mess the whole house up. In the past, this situation would have made me feel depressed, angry, frustrated, and downright defeated. My husband wouldn't even be moved by my emotions, but that didn't stop me from expressing them. Now, after many failed attempts of emotional manipulation, I use an approach that allows me to be a little more good-natured. I get to it when I can.

I had a friend ask me a very simple question, "Sis, Why does it make you so mad when he doesn't take initiative to clean up?... If he isn't worried, chill and get to it when you are ready...". This was a game-changer for me. I can't control my husband, but I can control how I respond to certain situations and to him. My goal now is to be kind and let things go. It's not always necessary to participate in arguments that you know you'll win. I don't always get it right, but I can feel God changing me into this woman... A self-controlled, good-natured woman.

Subject to their own husbands

Now, while the word says that a good woman is subject to her own husband, marriage itself is not a requirement to be considered pleasing to God. I want to start this by acknowledging that not everyone will end up married. I know that not everyone desires to be married, and that some women are no longer married. Being married doesn't make you any more or less valuable to God than you already are. For those of us who are married, we know that it requires releasing our independence and following the leadership of our husband. It's clear that we are not only to respect them, but to be subject to them. Being subject to your own husband is important to God. God stays on us because not only are we trying to get ourselves together, we are often walking through the process of another person getting their life together as well. That isn't always easy, especially when we don't choose well in the beginning. I don't say that in a prideful way, but the truth is that when we are broken we often choose broken men. This leads to us having to walk out God's word and subject ourselves under uncomfortable circumstances. For example, respecting a man that has not earned respect because God commands that you respect him anyway is hard, humbling work. Being subject to any human comes with challenges if we're honest. It requires trust, vulnerability, and willingness. It means following their leadership because you are not in charge.

 I admit that there were past seasons where I have been guilty of being more respectful and subject to a pastor than my own husband. I have been unconditionally respectful to my pastor, and felt justified in being disrespectful to my own husband because I was able to see his flaws on a daily basis. I eventually learned that not only was that displeasing to God, but that it caused my husband to harbor resentment. I would respect men that outranked me at work even if I didn't agree with them, but it was a struggle to submit to my own husband. That's something that I didn't even realize was happening, but now that I'm aware, I try my best to keep it in mind when I want to get out of line. To be subject means to show a form of obedience to your husband. When we are not subject to our husbands, it can make our lives and marriages challenging.

I see the opposite of being subject as trying to rule over your husband. Ruling over your husband looks like trying to control him and not allowing him to influence the direction of the family. This then causes us to end up demanding respect from our husbands, while in reality God has only called him to "love" us. If we are not careful, we will allow our unhealed souls to desire control of our husbands because of pride or a need for self-protection. Pride will deceive us into thinking that our thoughts and decisions are better than those of our husbands. Protection will convince us that controlling him ensures that we are not hurt, let down, or abandoned. I'm sure we can come up with a great reason for doing these things; however, those reasons do not make them godly. I felt my behavior was justified too, but I now know that it wasn't.

1 Peter 3:1-2 encourages us to be subject so that the word of God will not be dishonored. Just think about it. If our husbands see us praying, speaking in tongues, and being Holy Ghost filled while also exemplifying habitual qualities of Satan, he will not see a reason for taking us or God seriously. Yes, our husbands should want to serve the Lord on their own, but sometimes that just is not where he may. The word says, *"likewise, wives, be subject to your own husbands, so that even if some do not obey the word, they may be won without a word by the conduct of their wives, when they see your respectful and pure conduct (1 Peter 3:1-2 ESV)"*. This text tells us that the covenant of marriage requires us to be respectful and pure even if our husbands do not obey the word of God. In most cases, he wasn't obeying the Lord when we married him, but we try to force his journey as God starts to clean us up.

So, to my single ladies, consider whether or not your future mate is truly living for God in the beginning or be prepared to love him if he doesn't grow as quickly as you think he should. I have told several of my single friends that if you can't see yourself loving a man exactly the way he is now, don't marry him. No man is obligated to change just because you see his potential. Remember, You are going to be required to SUBJECT him. So, please be intentional in your dating season.

Ok, one last thing that I believe has deceived women is that many of us have been convinced that being "Sexy" indicates that we are good women. We may not say the words "I'm sexy, so respect me as a good woman", but I believe that at the core of us desiring to be sexy is the idea that it makes us more valuable. Sexy is defined as being sexually attractive or exciting. I hear women say all the time that there is nothing wrong with being sexy, and I agree to a certain extent. As a woman of God, we should be careful not to intentionally draw people to us in a sexual way. Many women are often upset when a man has sexual intentions based on the way a woman has presented herself. I know the world wants us to think it's ok to show it all, but the Bible actually speaks against it. "Like a gold ring in a pig's snout is a beautiful woman who shows no discretion." (Proverbs 11:22 NIV).

What is discretion? Discretion is the act of considering the consequences that our actions and decisions could lead to. If I show up on the blue app half-naked, I may draw unwanted sexual attention to myself because I have appealed to the sexual nature of men who may be attracted to me. I've seen women get online and publicly discuss all their sexual desires and preferences with no concern for how it will diminish their reputation. It takes self-control to know you are physically attractive, and yet choose not to use that as a way to gain attention. It takes discretion to know what is and is not public information. God is not concerned with our external beauty if our hearts and character are jacked up. He is calling us to be Holy women of God and that requires sacrifice and sometimes death to our old ways if they don't please God. It requires us to allow God to transform our minds with his Word. The more we read, the more our desire will be to please God. If you put on an outfit, and the first thing you say is "I look sexy", maybe you need to consider the root of the reason you are excited to look that way, especially if you're married. Don't get me wrong, I'm not saying that you shouldn't like the way you look. I know with great confidence that I'm attractive, but I've had to reprogram my mind to view myself with more depth when I look in the mirror.

I remember a time that I was offended by my husband saying he didn't like my clothes because they were so revealing. I didn't audibly call him insecure, but in my heart, that's what I was thinking. When I look back, that response was madness. He is my husband, and he knows how men think. He did not want me drawing unnecessary attention to myself because men often view women that lack discretion as attention-seeking. Ask yourself, how are you hyping yourself up? There's a big difference from when I used to say things to myself like "you're a bad bi***", and now reminding myself that I'm beautiful and that I'm fearfully and wonderfully made. God had to change my perspective. I don't dress the way I do because I'm worried about someone being attracted to me, but I do consider the type of attention I'm attracting. I have seen "women of God" speak boldly about the Lord and post videos pole dancing in booty shorts, and the saints were praising that behavior. That's an extreme example, but it's the reality that we live in. God gives us the freedom and liberty to do what we want, and as we allow His word to transform us, our desires should fall into alignment with His.

So take a few moments to evaluate yourself in this area. How do you present yourself to the world? Is it glorifying God or your flesh? When do you feel most confident? Can you feel confident when you're not showing every curve? If not, how can you get there? It starts with seeing all the beautiful aspects of yourself, to include your personality, your character, and your destiny. God doesn't limit purpose to those that fit the ideal standard of beauty. He uses those that have a heart for Him and that strive to walk in obedience to Him. If this resonated with you, please know that you are not alone. I was there and didn't even know it. Ask God to show you the reason you intentionally or unintentionally seek attention in that way. He will blow your mind. I saved this for last, because so many people will tell you that God doesn't care how you dress, and He doesn't. He is, however, concerned about your heart and intentions. He cares about the reasons you feel the need to show yourself in such an open way, and who you desire to please with your actions. In Romans, God tells us to present our bodies as living sacrifices, holy and acceptable, which is the least we can do (Romans 12:1). How are you presenting? To God and to the world? Take a minute to meditate on that scripture and allow God to speak to you. You will be amazed and humbled at what He has to say to your heart.

Whew Chile, that was a lot! This was the most challenging chapter for me to write if I'm being honest. I think it's because there is no specific definition of a good woman in the Bible, but we all know that God wants us to be godly. There are so many examples of godly and ungodly women that are being promoted. Some of the ungodly examples can be very tempting, but we have to examine those examples against God's word. When we begin to do that, we will clearly see what is and what is not of God. So while we may have lived our whole lives saved and sexy, it may be time to consider being a little more serious with God about what type of woman you are. He has called you to be godly, set apart, and to represent Him in places where people don't know God. If you look, behave, and think just like the world, what benefit is that to the kingdom? We are called to be the salt of the world and to make a difference. Don't lose your flavor, Sis. So go ahead... say it again... God, I'm serious this time!

"You are the salt of the earth; but if the salt loses its flavor, how shall it be seasoned? It is then good for nothing but to be thrown out and trampled underfoot by men. "You are the light of the world. A city that is set on a hill cannot be hidden. Nor do they light a lamp and put it under a basket, but on a lampstand, and it gives light to all who are in the house. Let your light so shine before men, that they may see your good works and glorify your Father in heaven. **Matthew 5:13-16** *(NKJV)*

Let's Pray.

God, thank you! Thank you for loving me enough to correct me, and at the same time loving me right where I am at this moment. You know everything about me. You know my thoughts and intentions. Help me to gain the right perspective of what it means to be a godly woman. I thank you in advance for changing my desires. In the name of Jesus, I bind the spirit of perversion that has been influencing my decisions. In the name of Jesus, I bind the spirit of pride that tries to convince me that there are areas of my life that are not important to you, and that there is no need for your input. I invite you into every area of my life. Change the way I speak if it doesn't please you! Change the way I think, dress, and eat if it doesn't please you. Purify me, and make me a mighty woman of God. I surrender myself to you as a living sacrifice. Help me to be holy and acceptable in Jesus' name. I want to give you glory with all of my life. So, purify me God and burn away anything that is not of you. From this moment forward, I declare that I am a godly woman!

In Jesus' Name, Amen!

Chapter 7

It's Serious This Time... Period!

11 For the grace of God has been revealed, bringing salvation to all people. 12 And we are instructed to turn from godless living and sinful pleasures. We should live in this evil world with wisdom, righteousness, and devotion to God, 13 while we look forward with hope to that wonderful day when the glory of our great God and Savior, Jesus Christ, will be revealed. 14 He gave his life to free us from every kind of sin, to cleanse us, and to make us his very own people, totally committed to doing good deeds.

Titus 2:11-15

You read it right, Sis! It's serious this time! Our commitment to serve the Lord is serious this time. No longer are we allowing the enemy to manipulate our wills and our lives. God's grace is more than enough to cover our shortcomings. What Jesus did on the cross is more than enough to cover us when we fall and pick us back up to try again. It's time to start evaluating the reasons we have been falling. It's time to reflect on our life, choices, relationships, behaviors, and purpose. Have we been unintentionally committed to carnal Christianity? Have we been more concerned about the things of this world than about the things of the spirit? Romans 8:5-6 (NKJV) says, *"For those who live according to the flesh set their minds on the things of the flesh, but those who live according to the Spirit, the things of the Spirit. For to be carnally minded is death, but to be spiritually minded is life and peace".* It's hard for us to recognize where we are if we don't know what God's word says about the flesh and the spirit. So many of us are participating in religion as usual because we don't recognize that our ways don't please God. In some cases, we know our ways don't please Him, but we still choose to do our own thing anyway. This often leads to fulfilling what our natural minds and bodies desire. Galatians 5:19-21 (NLT) says, *"When you follow the desires of your sinful nature (flesh), the results are very clear: sexual immorality, impurity, lustful pleasures, 20 idolatry, sorcery, hostility, quarreling, jealousy, outbursts of anger, selfish ambition, dissension, division, 21 envy, drunkenness, wild parties, and other sins like these".*

Let me tell you again as I have before, that anyone living that sort of life will not inherit the Kingdom of God."

Stop right here and examine yourself... not your friend, husband, or boss. Evaluate yourself! Do you find yourself doing these things the scripture mentions naturally or more often than you'd like? I know if I'm not mindful that I'll easily slip into selfish ambition, so I have to keep myself on a tight leash. The only reason I know this is that I've taken the time to get real with myself about the things that distract me from living the way God intends. Yes, He wants me to have goals, but He also wants those goals to glorify Him and be in alignment with His will. So, I spend time asking myself if my plans are more pleasing to God or to Whittney when I am making big plans for my life. The word says a man's heart has many plans, but the Lord's purpose will prevail (Proverbs 19:21). Keeping this at the forefront of my mind helps me to avoid making my life all about me and more about God. So, what's something you have to keep a tight leash on? What are the areas of your life that you know you need deliverance from? What are the things keeping you from being serious with God? He already knows, He's just waiting on you to acknowledge it. When you look back over the past year of your life, what has been the common theme for you spiritually? Is it the same theme that's been lingering for the past 5 years? That testimony ends for you this year!

Your Enemy

Even though this guy is already defeated, he does a great job convincing us of the opposite. When we are not in our right, renewed minds, he is able to manipulate us into believing what we see instead of what we KNOW. He's literally waiting to catch you slipping. 1 Peter 5:8 says, *"Be clear-headed. Keep alert. Your accuser, the devil, is on the prowl like a roaring lion, seeking someone to devour."* Sis, I don't know about you, but my years of being devoured are over. There were times in my life that I ran into the trap of the enemy, but these days, I refuse to make the enemy's victory easy. God is warning us to be alert.

Alert is defined as quick to notice any unusual and potentially dangerous or difficult circumstances. How alert are you? Do you recognize when the enemy is trying to attack? Are you leading yourself into traps by living unintentionally? Let's be real, if you are consumed with toxic relationships, friendships, substances, procrastination, overconsumption, and social media, then it's gonna be hard to stay alert. If we keep ourselves tied down with these things, the enemy doesn't have to work very hard to devour us because WE destroy ourselves. We have been given power over the enemy (Luke 10:19). We have weapons that we probably aren't even using. Instead of complaining, we should be praying. Instead of worrying, we should be trusting in God. Instead of carrying ours and everyone else's problems, we should be casting them on Jesus. If you are expecting the weekly visit to church to sustain you in battle the entire week, Sis, you should honestly expect to lose. Warriors don't train one day a week for battle. They don't listen to one motivational speech and then go out and attempt to win wars. They train and prepare. Have you been training? Have you been preparing? If the answer is no, why do you expect to win? Sis, it's time out for weekly encounters with God and daily encounters with satan. From the time we leave the church, Satan is bombarding us with his people, music, TV shows, and all sorts of other temptations. Instead of accepting that as normal, it's time to start intentionally blocking his access to us.

Get your people, places, and things in check. The people we connect with, the places we go, and the things we do all need to be in alignment with God. Being intentional about those things will build our spiritual arsenals for the wars we may encounter throughout the day. The enemy is well aware of the power and authority we have in Christ Jesus; he's just hoping that we choose not to use it. He knows that as soon as we get bold enough to cast him out and rebuke him in the name of Jesus, it's over. So his objective is to keep us broken, depressed, stressed, angry, and unforgiving so that he can maintain his access to our lives. But the minute we make a conscious decision to turn away from those things in repentance, we instantly level up! We are no longer on the same level. We have to remember that even the newest believer in Jesus Christ is more powerful than the highest person in the kingdom of darkness. The Bible says that at the name of Jesus EVERY knee must bow... (Philippians 2:10). The same power that was working in Jesus when he cast out demons and healed the sick is the same power working in us through the Holy Spirit. It's time for us to start acting like we know the spiritual weight we carry.

So, it's time Sis. Get the sin out of your life. Ask God to help you clean up the meditations of your heart. Ask Him to help you make the words of your mouth acceptable in His sight. Give everything that belongs to Satan back to him. It's time for you to start moving like you know you belong to the winning team. Regardless of what you see happening!

Where's Your Armor Sis?

As a soldier in the Army, I can't imagine sending my troops into battle without their weapons and armor. Imagine my entire unit heading into Talil, Iraq, with no weapons, no protective vests, no combat helmets, into buildings with no protective barriers. We would be easy targets for Iraqi insurgents. So, in the same way, we are easy targets for Satan's army when we refuse to put on our armor due to ignorance, laziness, or rebellion. Are you an easy target, Sis? Are you or those you love constantly attacked by the enemy because you failed to put on the full armor of God? If you are going to take a serious stance against the kingdom of darkness, you're gonna have to strap up. First, let's make sure we're clear on what the armor is.

What is the armor of God?

> *Wherefore take unto you the whole armor of God, that ye may be able to withstand in the evil day, and having done all, to stand. 14 Stand therefore, having your loins girt about with truth, and having on the breastplate of righteousness; 15 And your feet shod with the preparation of the gospel of peace; 16 Above all, taking the shield of faith, wherewith ye shall be able to quench all the fiery darts of the wicked. 17 And take the helmet of salvation, and the sword of the Spirit, which is the word of God. 18 Praying always with all prayer and supplication in the Spirit, and watching thereunto with all perseverance and supplication for all saints."*
> **Ephesians 6:13–18 (KJV)**

The first thing we are told to do is stand. At first, I almost skipped over this word, but I'm glad I didn't because it's important. Here, we are encouraged to continue standing when we have done all that we can in our own strength. To stand biblically means to remain firm and immovable. At this moment in the scripture, we're not being commanded to charge or attack, but to simply stand. It's as though we are a resting place for God's supernatural armor to do all the work.

Have you ever seen someone design a character in a combat video game? The character is standing there while the creator places all the armor on them. After they are dressed, the person using the controller does all the work. The character is simply the chosen vessel for the mission. That's how I see God using us in spiritual battle. When we put on the armor, He is capable of using us to accomplish his missions in the earth as He guides our actions.

While standing, we are to have our loins girded about with the belt of truth. This is a fancy way of saying prepare ourselves for difficulties and challenges by standing on truth. We are not called to stand in our own truth, our friend's truth, or our pastor's truth, but God's truth. Biblical truth is consistent with the mind, will, character, glory, and being of God. The belt holds up other weapons and protects our private areas from being exposed. When who we are and what we do are founded on truth, we don't have to worry about lies and secrets being exposed due to a faulty belt (lies). We can rest confidently knowing that we have everything we need for battle.

The breastplate of righteousness is given to help protect us from the attacks of the enemy and sin. Sin is literally everywhere, and if we are not careful, our very own body can work against us in this area. Righteousness is defined as the quality of being right in the eyes of God, including character (nature), conscience (attitude), conduct (action), and command (obedience to His word). When we don't put on the breastplate (righteousness), by default, we are left in our flesh, which is naturally sinful. Our flesh will have us out here doing things that are in complete opposition to what God desires for us. The breastplate protects some of the most vital organs. It protects your heart, lungs, and other life-sustaining functions. I can't even count all the times my unrighteousness has led to my heart being broken. Some of my decisions have left me feeling breathless from chasing things that were unrighteous and not in God's will for my life. I've made countless decisions based on emotions and unwise counsel rather than seeking God or His word. Listen Sis, this breastplate recommendation is serious. The Bible instructs us to "put on" the breastplate because it is a daily choice. The same way that we wake up and put on clothes is the same way we must wake up and choose to put on righteousness. When we wake up and put on songs about sin and drama, we are choosing to allow those things to influence our moods, minds, and attitudes for the day. If the person we are listening to is dealing with anger, lust, or low self-esteem, we can expect for those things to creep into our moods as well. These are subtle, sneaky ways that sin and unrighteousness give Satan access to our lives. So, our goal is to grow and mature in God; righteousness is something we have to make a part of who we are by choosing to put it on every day. One thing I've learned is that the more we ask God to search and clean up our hearts, the more desire we cultivate for righteousness. The more we guard our hearts from toxic, ungodly things, the easier it is for us to recognize when ungodly stuff has crept in. The Bible even tells us to guard our hearts with all diligence because from it flow the issues of life (Proverbs 4:23).

Are you guarding your heart, Sis? Are you selective about what you concern yourself with, what you love, who you love, and what you devote your attention to? If you haven't been intentional about it, here's a friendly reminder... choose to put on RIGHTEOUSNESS.

Now, I know everyone didn't grow up in the country, walking barefoot on rocks and hot asphalt like me. But, I'm sure y'all can imagine stepping on pointy rocks and feeling the intense heat, and trying your best to find an alternate path to walk without shoes. Sometimes, life feels like walking outside without shoes. One minute, the beautiful green grass seems harmless, and then bam! You step on a sharp rock and start rethinking your entire decision to dash out of the door without your shoes on. Throughout this walk with God, I've learned that the unexpected rocks are inevitable. I realize that whether I was intentionally walking with God or rebelliously doing my own thing, challenges still came. The difference was simply how I approached them. I didn't know at the time, but walking through things God's way yields a different perspective in the midst of challenges.

Paul says, *"And your feet shod with the preparation of the gospel of peace"* (**Ephesians 6:15 KJV**).

A "shod" is basically a shoe. The shoes that he's insisting we put on as we walk our Christian journey are *the preparation of the gospel of peace*. I don't know about you, but Whittney B.C. (before Christ) didn't have peace in anything. Like seriously, the smallest struggle would have me bent out of shape. I wasn't concerned about preparing the gospel for my use, nor was I conscious of the option for peace in difficult situations. I had normalized surviving without spiritual shoes in earlier seasons of my life. Today, I'm a little more conscious of my option to walk in peace when things start to get crazy. I always have the option to start worrying or stay discouraged for longer than I should, but what comes out of that? I'm trying to get to the peace that Jesus had when he was asleep on the boat while the sea was going crazy. When everyone else was afraid of dying in the storm, Jesus took their worry as a lack of faith saying, "*how is it that you have no faith?*".

The disciples knew that Jesus was with them, and still fell into being afraid. This lets me know that it's possible for us to know that Christ is with us, and give in to fear due to what it looks like. Can you imagine them sitting on the boat, waves hitting them upside the head, yet remaining unbothered... it would have looked like peace. This kind of peace comes from being prepared in the gospel. We can't get this kind of peace by only reading our Word and praying once a week. This kind of peace is gained through knowing God, and we get to know Him through His word. So, check your shoes Sis. No more walking spiritually barefoot on this journey. It's time for us to shod our feet with the preparation of the gospel of peace, and refuse to walk without it. Lace up Sis! We're sure to hit some rough terrain, but with the right spiritual shoes you will be ready.

Now I know that we've got our spiritual shoes on and can't wait to walk in peace when the next challenge presents itself, but there's more. God ain't sending us into battle empty-handed. While He knows we're prepared to maintain our peace, there are some things He wants us to avoid completely, so He has given us a *shield of faith*. In verse 16, Paul says, *"Above all, taking the shield of faith, wherewith ye shall be able to quench all the fiery darts of the wicked".* Having peace doesn't mean that fiery darts will not attempt to kill and destroy us. A shield blocks and protects us from close and long-range attacks. In biblical days, the shield would often cover the soldier's entire body and serve as a barrier that could be used to push back the enemy in close combat. The Lord lets us know that the enemy goes beyond attacking with basic arrows. He even has the audacity to make them fiery! I know this is no lie because without faith, some of the stuff I've been through felt like my entire life was set on fire. Come to find out, the devil was just out here freely lighting me up with fiery darts because I had no faith. There was nothing blocking the attack of the darts! The Word says that the shield of faith *quenches or extinguishes* all the fiery attacks of the enemy. That perspective completely changed the way I live now.

The devil tries to tell me I'm going to hell for the abortion I had, but my faith blocks that lie and reassures me that I am forgiven (1 John 1:9). My feelings try to convince me to hold on to the hurt caused by someone I loved, but my faith says forgive because God has forgiven me (Ephesians 4:32). Sickness tries to overtake my body, but my faith reminds me that by His stripes I am healed (Isaiah 53:5). My husband and children start acting like God is irrelevant, but I speak in faith regardless of what it looks like. As for me and my house, we will serve the Lord (Joshua 24:15). And let me be clear, faith isn't simply speaking these things. It's BELIEVING these things. Faith is refusing to accept what things look like in the natural. It's remembering that before a seed sprouts things are taking place beneath the surface. It's planting as many seeds as we can with our words, watering those seeds with our actions, and waiting for God to bring the increase when HE sees fit. I'm talking about the kind of faith that made Daniel and his friends walk into a furnace that was seven times hotter than normal, knowing that whether or not God delivered them, He was still God (Daniel 3:16-18). Those men had faith. They trusted their God to the point of death. Whew... now that's a shield of faith! So my point here is that fiery darts are gonna come. Girl, it may even feel like you're being thrown into a fiery furnace, but faith shields you from it all. Make a commitment to growing your faith. The Bible says that faith comes by hearing, and hearing the Word of God (Romans 10:17). Be intentional about hearing the word of God.

Now, while we are talking about hearing the word of God, don't overlook the fact that our ears are on our head. Verse 17 says, *"And take the helmet of salvation, and the sword of the Spirit, which is the word of God".* Can you imagine going into battle without a helmet? Maybe you can't, but as a Soldier in the US Army, I know that one thing we always have on when going into battle is our helmet. It's so important because it protects the command station for the body. If someone suffers a non-fatal blow or shot to the head, the rest of the armor is useless, much like our spiritual lives. If our minds are not protected from the fiery darts of the enemy (and he has a lot of them), we won't even attempt to use the armor on our bodies. But why is it referred to as the *"helmet of Salvation"*?

I think it's because having your salvation at the forefront of your mind is a constant reminder of your identity in Christ. The same way football helmets identify a team, our helmet of salvation lets the kingdom of darkness know who we belong to. Salvation is defined as deliverance from sin and its consequences, by having faith in Christ. Our salvation gives us access to all the other armor. Without salvation, there is no faith, unless you're talking about faith in self or worldly things. Remembering our salvation helps to dictate how we live our life. The command station has to be protected at all times because it informs our bodies how to navigate the world. How many times have you gotten caught slipping when you forgot about your salvation, or set it aside to do what you wanted? When we live like we have not been saved, it leads to sin and ultimately, death. We may even keep living physically, but spiritually we will be dying. So, putting on the helmet of salvation is vital to preventing the enemy from infiltrating our minds and thoughts. Where's your helmet? Do you have it on, or have you taken it off without realizing that one of your most vital body parts is exposed to the enemy? If you find yourself being more negative, doubtful, anxious, or depressed, it's time to find your helmet, Sis.

I instantly started visualizing myself as a ninja as I got ready to tell y'all about the sword of the spirit. I know, crazy right lol. Listen, I'm for real though. We have to be ninjas in the spirit. If the Lord says the Word of God is like a sword, then baby, just go ahead and call me a demon slayer, because it's bound to get real. Ok, but seriously, why are we told to view the word of God as a sword of the Spirit? A sword can be used offensively to attack and defensively to protect. Hebrews 4:12 says, *"For the word of God is alive and active. Sharper than any double-edged sword, it penetrates even to dividing soul and spirit, joints and marrow; it judges the thoughts and attitudes of the heart".* That's a powerful sword, and it's so necessary for this spiritual battle that we are fighting.

Why is it so important for the word to be able to divide the soul and spirit? Our souls are made up of our mind, will, and emotions. Our minds control how we think. Our will is what we choose to do and the decisions we make. Finally, our emotions are the way we express what we are feeling. The soul is influenced by our environment, family, friends, society, values, and entertainment. We didn't just pop out of our mother's womb looking for our zodiac signs. We were probably encouraged or discouraged to read them by the people in our environments, families, friend groups, or someone we follow on social media. Our souls are the internal part of us that drives our physical bodies. It alone shouldn't control us, but sometimes our minds and emotions will lead us to use our wills to do things that are not okay with God. Our spirit, on the other hand, is the part of us that connects with God.

When we accept Jesus Christ, we receive the gift of the Holy Spirit. The Holy Spirit attempts to lead and guide us so that we use our wills to please God. If we don't take proper care of our souls, our emotions can lead us to operate based on how we feel, rather than what the Word of God says. For example, someone may intentionally hurt or offend us with no remorse. Our souls may lead us to think that it's acceptable to hold a grudge and not forgive, but now that the Holy Spirit lives inside of us, there's a requirement to forgive. Simply reading God's word helps us to separate our souls from our spirits. Ephesians 4:30-32 (NKJV) says, *"And do not grieve the Holy Spirit of God, by whom you were sealed for the day of redemption. Let all bitterness, wrath, anger, clamor, and evil speaking be put away from you, with all malice. And be kind to one another, tenderhearted, forgiving one another, even as God in Christ forgave you."* Whew... The sword comes in and shows us that separating our souls from our spirits is necessary to make good decisions. The Word of God judges the thoughts and intentions of our hearts, so that we are not destroying ourselves. Anger, resentment, bitterness, and unforgiveness all sabotage our spiritual life and make it harder for us to use our sword against the enemy, because we are then too busy tending to our own self-inflicted wounds. When we allow God's word to change us, we can then use the sword to defend ourselves against the enemy. Quoting scriptures in the heat of trials reminds us and the devil who has the victory. We can use the Bible to identify and heal the areas of our hearts and minds that give the enemy access to kill, steal, and destroy our hope and confidence in God.

Can you imagine trying to fight an actual war without a weapon? In the same way, we cannot attempt to fight spiritual battles without God's word. I'm sorry to tell you this, but our words are not enough, Sis. If we are going to fight effectively, we must have our weapon on us at all times. The devil doesn't have office hours. He isn't going to tell us when the attack is coming. The only way we will be ready at all times is by being ready at all times. The Bible tells us to hide the Word of God in our hearts so that we don't sin against it (Psalm 119:11). I may not be able to tell you the exact scripture for all the verses hidden in my heart, but there are a ton of them in my heart. The more I read the Bible and take it as the true and living Word, the more I don't want to forget it. These biblical principles that I read have become a part of who I am and what I stand for. I try my best not to disrespect my husband because God's word tells me not to. I don't know every scripture reference for this by heart, but the principle is a part of who I am as a woman. I only got to that point because I studied it and really took it to heart when I learned better. My point here is that by reading the Bible as a Christian, not only do we get to know God, but we are equipped with weapons that will outdo any man-made contraption of the human mind.

So, we've discussed all the physical metaphors of our spiritual armor, and God left the ultimate part of our armor for the very end. Instead of using a metaphor, He simply instructed us to pray. As we approach the subject of prayer, I'm mind blown at how God is so strategic and intentional in everything that He does. In the last eight months, He has put a fire in me to pray more than I ever have in my life. The way that prayer has transformed my relationship with God is joyously overwhelming, and I want the same joy for you. My renewed call to prayer started with God nudging me at 3 am to pray. His bidding became so obvious that I could not, and did not want to ignore it. I didn't know it at the time, but He was calling me to a closer, more intimate relationship with Him, and He was calling me to be an intercessor.

So much of our spiritual warfare is won and shifted in prayer. We serve the God of the angel armies. Psalms 89:8-9 (NLT) says *"God of the Angel Armies, who is like you, powerful and faithful from every angle? 9 You put the arrogant ocean in its place and calm its waves when they turn unruly".* So, every time I pray, I gain confidence that I am on the winning team during battle. Have you seen the ocean roaring? To serve a God that has the power to calm it should settle any doubts that try to rise up in our minds. Prayer is the access point that we use to tap into the spiritual resources outside of ourselves. In actual combat, attack helicopters don't randomly drop bombs. People in battle call the ones with the air support capability and tell them when and where to attack. That is the same authority we have in spiritual warfare. Some of us are fighting when we should be praying and calling in the next level of strength, power, and attack from above.

What happens if Soldiers never call for fire? What happens if we never call on God in prayer to handle our situation? We end up trying to do battle on our own. We may even end up feeling overwhelmed and burned out. We must remember that God was so strategic about equipping us for warfare, so He left nothing out. Yes, we can attempt to war on our own and with others, but why would we do so when we have access to the God of the angel armies? We'd be fools not to use the extra support. I've found myself forgetting about this level of support in the middle of a battle. I've spent countless hours thinking and strategizing instead of praying. These days, I'm having to train my mind to pray instead of trying to make it all make sense because some things just won't make sense to my natural mind. We must realize that there's an invisible spiritual battle going on that takes spiritual weapons and strategy that only God can provide. Yeah, we can see some things going on in front of us, but what's going on in the spiritual realm simultaneously? We are not helpless! We can use our spiritual weapon of prayer as a way to prevent the enemy from being successful at attacking certain areas of our lives. This principle is really powerful when you think about it, so take advantage of it. Pray without ceasing (1 Thessalonians 5:17). The devil trembles at the thought of God answering our prayers because his objective is to get us to doubt their effectiveness. Remember Sis, just because we don't see anything happening naturally doesn't mean that God's not moving spiritually. So, put on the full armor of God, and don't take it off!

Spend Time with God

So, I'm challenging you, just as I'm challenging myself, to pray. Pray without ceasing. Turn off the noise, sermons, audiobooks, and pray so that you can hear God's voice more clearly. He wants to speak to us, but we must be willing to get in a position to hear. It's really hard to hear when our environments are loud. Don't get me wrong, the things we may be listening to are probably helpful and there's a time for all those things. We just can't allow those things to take the place of God. I have found myself consuming so many sermons, books, and podcasts, but spending minimal time talking and hearing from God. My intentions were good, but I also found myself referring to the words of my favorite teacher instead of God's word because I was so filled with their interpretations and perspectives (which were all valid).

I'm really trying to drive home our need to spend quality time with God. It's our need as His creation to commune with Him. It's a need for us to get to know Him. We don't build trust with humans without getting to know them, so why do we expect to know and trust God without spending intimate time with Him? I'm not suggesting that we'll ever fully comprehend all of God, but the more we read His Word, the more we learn to trust that we can depend on Him. After all these years, I have just now evolved to spend intimate time with God consistently. For me, that looks like waking up early while my house is quiet and spending time with my Father. Sometimes my flesh tries to convince me to sleep in, but my spirit quickly reminds me of the need to get up. The crazy thing is that no matter how tired I am, the presence of God gives me so much energy and strength. Instead of looking at the time as something lost, it's now something that adds to my day. Listen, when you get started it may feel a little forced. You may feel awkward, sleepy, and unsure of what to pray for. But, press in! If you keep showing up, God will speak to you, and His presence will become more natural and desired.

Allowing ourselves to silence the voices of our favorite humans forces us to spend time with ourselves. It makes space for us to check in with our thoughts and submit them to God. We also get a chance to hear from God for creativity and vision. Silence is really a good thing when we normalize it in our life. So ask yourself this question... Do I intentionally spend time with God? If it has not been a priority, then I encourage you to take a small, realistic step to start today. You can begin with 15 minutes with God and work your way up as God leads you. Choose a time to read the Bible, pray, or read a devotional, and then take a few moments to consider what God may be trying to say to you. I'm telling you Sis, time with God is where it's at! This is the secret place we hear the older saints talking about. I'm so glad that God has shown me this now, so that I can continue to grow closer to God in this season of my life. This is the driving force behind our ability to get serious about God. Knowing Him for ourselves.

Are You Ready to Get Serious?

It's a question you really need to ask yourself. Are you truly ready to get serious about your relationship with God? What makes this time different? Why is it so necessary for you to get close to the one who pre-planned and knows your destiny? What have you been missing out on by avoiding this pivotal part of your life and purpose trajectory? I'll suggest one reason, and prayerfully more reasons will begin to overwhelm your mind with possibilities.

So here it is! God has ALWAYS had a plan and purpose for our lives! Before our moms and dads even came together, HE HAD A PLAN FOR US. God had a plan that would help glorify Him and His kingdom. Jeremiah 1:5 (NIV) says, *"Before I formed you in the womb I knew you, before you were born I set you apart; I appointed you as a prophet to the nations".* Don't let the *prophet to the nations* part scare you. When we seek God, He will show us the specific purpose He has for us. It is our job to believe that God has a purpose for our lives. There are so many circumstances that attempt to distract us from realizing that purpose. Hardships, family dynamics, trauma, generational curses, and doubt are a few examples. My hope is that by now we are more aware of the enemy's attempts to distract us from knowing God's plan for our lives. God desires good things for us. Through Christ, we have the ability to start seeking what God desires of us so that everything else can be added to our lives (Matthew 6:33). So, this is my charge to you.

No matter where you are in life, seek the kingdom of God and His righteousness. Seek God for what it means to be Holy and righteous. The word gives clear instructions, so look to it for guidance and clarity. If you've been saved for a long time, this is your sign to elevate your commitment to God. It's time to seek Him for wisdom and guidance on how we can walk out the charge of Titus 2. We need strong believers in all phases of life. We should not allow things like race, location, and age to separate us. Instead, our differences should show the Glory of God that allows us to unite across differences in order to serve a true and living God. Living by the Spirit of God secures our eternity and connects us with others who can walk with us during our time here on earth. You don't have to do this thing alone. In fact, God encourages us to come together even more as we get closer to Christ's return

(Hebrews 10:25). He knew that coming together with other believers would encourage us on the journey.

Social media brings the whole world to our palms, and it can appear that evil is prevailing. Seeing so much negativity and evil at work can discourage our desire for holiness and endurance in the faith. Being around other believers helps us to refocus and gain strength, knowing that we are not alone on the narrow path of faith. So, I exhort you to seek God. Really get to know your Father. Read your word, commit to prayer, and right living as much as you can. My prayer is that God will hear your declaration and meet you right where you are in this moment. This is the moment you will intentionally and genuinely confess... God, I'm Serious This Time!

Let's Pray.

Lord, thank you for giving my sister a desire to get serious about her relationship with you. Thank you for speaking to her heart about the plans and desires that you have for her life. God, I pray that you will silence every lie that the enemy attempts to tell her. I pray that she will only hear your voice. Take away every desire that prevents her from getting closer to you. Give her confidence in your Word. Allow her to read and believe it with her whole heart. Give her wisdom and understanding as she reads your Word. Let your Word change the way she thinks, speaks, and acts. God, we ask that you would break every generational curse hovering over her life, in Jesus' name. We praise you for the plan and the destiny that you've had for her since before she was formed in her mother's womb. As she begins to seek your kingdom and your righteousness, add everything she needs to her life. Allow her to put on the whole armor of God every day. Allow her to prioritize intimate time with you so that she can grow in discerning your voice. May she seek you for guidance in every situation, and trust that through Christ all things are possible. I thank you in advance for the work she will do in the kingdom of God. Bless her life, and use her for your glory! God, we come into agreement that she is serious this time!

In Jesus' Name, Amen!

Whew!! You made it through Sis!

Now let's talk Community & Resources...

I'm so proud of you for finishing the book, and hopefully you've gained a greater desire for intimacy with God. I know personally how important community is when it comes to lasting change. If you're ready to find some women with like minds, consider joining my Facebook community! It's called **The Intentional Woman Safe Space**. I host weekly zoom bible studies and prayer calls. We have girl nights where we come together on zoom to discuss navigating the world as bold Women of God. Basically, it's a good time Sis. Scan the QR code below to join us, and to find links to my YouTube channel and podcast. See you over there!

Whittney K

REFERENCES

Demons & Magic Sermon – John Macarthur 1973

https://www.gty.org/library/sermons-library/1218/demons-and-magic

A Complete Guide to Biblical Fasting: Master the Habit that Provokes God's favor. Ted Shuttlesworth

https://a.co/d/5o4XIG8

The Willie Lynch Letter and The Making of A Slave

Willie Lynch and Haile Gerima (February 28, 1999)

Destroying the Spirit of Rejection – John Eckhardt

Alpha Kappa Alpha Ritual Circa 1977